# Collaborating For Success

## LEARN HOW TO BUILD HIGH PERFORMANCE COLLABORATIVE TEAMS

## Paul Williams

Grosvenor House
Publishing Limited

This book is published by
Grosvenor House Publishing Ltd
28-30 High Street, Guildford, Surrey, GU1 3HY.
www.grosvenorhousepublishing.co.uk

A CIP record for this book
is available from the British Library

ISBN 978-1-78148-383-1

# CONTENTS

Contents

Contents

# WHO I AM AND WHAT THIS BOOK IS ABOUT

I am Paul Williams, and I have been studying and providing guidance and advice on people-related issues across a number of industries for over 30 years.

This short book is a distillation of my experience in joining groups together to create truly high performance teams. These groups might comprise functions within the same organisation, clients with their suppliers, or groups from different countries. The common theme is that, even if it is difficult, it is imperative to create a true 'one-team' feel in order to produce a high performance culture.

This book is concerned with the concepts behind creating high performance collaborative teams, and looks at collaboration, organisational culture, management of change, the characteristics of high performance teams and how people can attain true excellence. It deals as much, if not more, with people-related issues as it does with processes and procedures, since it is people issues that are the key to the attainment of high levels of performance; however, these are often marginalised in a desire to focus on the more familiar issues concerning procedures and processes.

I have tried to introduce the concepts and issues in an interesting, pragmatic and readable way, and I hope that reading this book will help you shape both your own thinking and your plans for the future.

My own view is that most aspects of life are simply about decisions, consequences and memories. I hope that you feel you have made the right decision to read this book, and that as a consequence it will leave you with positive, helpful and enlightening memories.

If you would like to contact me after reading this book to continue a collaborative discussion my email is paulwilliams@wcgcollaboration.com

# 1

## WHAT IS COLLABORATION?

### It's Not New

Collaboration between people and groups is clearly not a novelty. For centuries people have, either by desire or necessity, sought to interact to achieve a common goal, be it for personal reasons, group survival, commercial success or sporting achievements.

Technological advances have now made collaboration easier, but it has to be remembered that collaboration is different to the interactions generated by the current proliferation of social media such as Facebook and Twitter. Collaboration has a specifically defined purpose which has been agreed upon by the parties interacting, and is intended to satisfy this objective.

### Collaboration is Natural

Collaboration is a natural progression in the communication process. In my lifetime I have seen a transition from letters to telexes, faxes, emails and video conferencing (VC) connectivity; now, recent technological advances mean it is possible for remote groups to be joined together via visual, audio and data connectivity to produce one virtual team. This provides an organisation with the opportunity for a true paradigm shift, enabling everyone to challenge existing processes and procedures and create revolutionary new ways of working, leading to productivity improvements.

## Dealing with People Issues

Effective collaboration depends upon:

- installing the appropriate technology
- creating the right physical environment
- developing new organisational structures, processes and procedures
- developing appropriate behaviours
- creating an appropriate culture.

My own experience is that most organisations feel more comfortable and able to deal with activities which are not people-related – activities where they can design, document and implement any required modifications or changes under logical, controlled conditions. This is particularly applicable in industrial, manufacturing and technologically-driven organisations. However, such organisations can lack the ability to effectively deal with the 'softer' people issues which arise. These require the consideration of:

- emotions
- feelings
- prejudices
- relationships
- behaviours.

In many organisations, leaders often delegate people issues to the HR (human resources) function, which in reality is wholly inappropriate. Although HR may provide a valuable resource to deal with conditions of employment, it should not be held accountable or responsible for the development of appropriate individual behaviours, nor relationships between individuals within teams. This should be the responsibility of the appointed leader.

## Searching for the Answer

Throughout my career, I have seen numerous new techniques, processes and systems developed to help improve the efficiency of organisations, ranging from Terotechnology, Just-In-Time, Business Process Redesign, Lean Manufacturing and Kaizen, to name but a few. These are all laudable techniques to introduce new ways of working in order to improve operational and organisational efficiency for commercial advantage, but they often ignore the human element, and certainly don't deal with collaboration.

Many years ago, I was involved in a number of governmental quangos looking at why the UK's manufacturing efficiency lagged behind that of other developed countries, especially Japan. Numerous fact-finding missions looked for the reasons behind Japan's attainment of higher efficiency levels, which resulted in the production of heavy tomes containing technical details that were eventually woven into white papers for dissemination amongst industry leaders. All the papers, however, failed to either identify or accept that perhaps the main reason for the attainment of higher efficiency levels in Japan was the diligence, attentiveness and work ethic of the workforce – maybe this was not highlighted as it was too painful to admit to!

## It's Not Just Another Technique

Collaborative working is not just another efficiency improvement technique or tool, but an enabler for creating one truly effective and efficient team. However, joining people together from different groups, who have different ways of working and who have individual mindsets, is not an easy process. It requires individuals to develop new allegiances and possibly have their own ideas and views challenged; this can cause natural resistance, leading to organisational dissonance.

In helping organisations to develop and implement collaborative working, my experience has shown that dealing with people issues is not only important but critical, yet I have found that these people issues are almost always relegated to the end of any agenda, be it concerning the design, development or implementation of any change programme. When it does eventually come to 'people issues', I have witnessed many a meeting where laptops are suddenly opened or hands disappear beneath the desk to check emails and texts on smartphones – possibly a none-too-subtle indication of the level of interest or importance placed on dealing with the softer issues of collaboration.

A contributing factor in putting people issues at the end of many agendas is probably discomfort in articulating and dealing with emotional, relationship and behavioural issues. In early engagement workshops designed to talk about collaboration, I have often asked those with teenage children how emotionally connected they feel they are to them. It transpires that the adults' ability to connect with their own children has gradually diminished over time – they often feel they lack the language to relate to them, and so feel uncomfortable with emotional conversations. It is therefore no surprise that, when creating collaborative environments whose success relies upon surfacing and dealing with relationship issues, people issues are sidelined, ignored or simply paid lip-service to.

This book is designed to address this head on. It is solely about the people issues that need to be dealt with in joining groups together so that individuals can collaborate effectively and harmoniously to create high performance teams. There are no right or wrong answers, and there are no convenient templates which can be populated and applied. This book purely raises the topics that need to be addressed and provides the reader with an understanding of these issues, together with suggestions about how they might be tackled. The precise interventions required will, however, depend upon the existing attitudes, behaviours and mindsets of the groups being joined together in the pursuit of creating truly high performance teams.

## A New Capability

It is also important to recognise and remember that collaboration is a new capability that individuals have the freedom to decide how and when to deploy. It cannot, therefore, be dictated or enforced; instead, individuals have to understand the potential of the capability and decide how to apply it themselves.

As we will see later, this element of choice means that the design and implementation of a change programme to embed collaborative working in any organisation relies heavily on individuals understanding the power of the capability and then deciding for themselves how it can be utilised. Hence, any implementation programme must be heavily biased towards educating people on the underlying concepts, rather than relying on traditional process-managed implementation programmes.

Collaboration depends upon successful, harmonious interactions with a wide variety of people from different backgrounds and experiences who may well see the world from different perspectives. This may mean letting go of opinions that help unite co-located groups and seeing the other group's point of view. This enables them to see another group, which might once have been perceived as 'the enemy', as valuable colleagues.

## Don't Forget to Collaborate at Every Level in the Organisation!

We will be moving on to look at the benefits of collaboration and how groups can be joined together. There is, however, an inherent danger that, when joining groups together, the teams are united by enabling technologies, meaning that they can interact on a real-time basis, but that this does not necessarily extend to their senior managers, who are hence separated by a 'collaboration gap'.

This results in understanding and alignment between the different teams, but creates the danger of misunderstanding between them and their senior managers, whose team members are being influenced by other groups, possibly without their knowledge; this can come as a surprise and lead to feelings of loss of control. This is illustrated in the diagram opposite.

| KEY MESSAGES |
| --- |
| • Collaboration is a natural progression |
| • Don't delegate people-related issues – embrace them |
| • In developing collaborative working, don't put people issues last on any agenda |
| • Don't sideline, marginalise or trivialise people issues |
| • Collaboration is a new capability, and individuals need to decide how to apply it for maximum benefit |
| • Ensure people understand the concepts behind collaboration |
| • Embrace new perspectives and let go of stereotypes |
| • Collaborate at all levels in the organisation |

# 2

# Benefits of Collaboration

## New Communication Systems

The introduction of any new communication system or process brings with it a range of benefits that will be the rationale behind it, provide a number of business advantages, and help the organisation potentially achieve improvements in operational performance and efficiency.

However, it is also true that every new communication system or process brings with it a number of disadvantages that need to be identified and managed. Clearly, if the disadvantages are sufficiently significant and serious, it would be appropriate to evaluate how they might be mitigated; and, indeed, if they outweigh the advantages, it is important to assess the wisdom of adopting the new communication system or process at all.

For example, the introduction of mobile phones brought the tangible and obvious advantage of being able to contact anyone at any time, but also an attendant disadvantage: the risk of being constantly disturbed. People therefore quickly learned to cope with this disadvantage by utilising messaging, alerts and diverts, or turning their phones off when they did not want to be disturbed.

Another disadvantage of the latest communication systems, be they mobile phones, laptops or tablets, is that people feel the need to respond immediately to an incoming call, text or email, even in meetings, so diverting their attention from what is being discussed. It is quite astounding how this habit has become virtually endemic in most organisations, accepted as common practice and not perceived for what it is – disruptive, inefficient and discourteous to others at the meeting. How many times have we all witnessed a question directed at someone who has had their attention diverted by another form of communication, only to be met with the response, "Sorry, what did you say?"

Curiously, this was vividly demonstrated to me a few years ago when queuing at a hotel reception to ask for directions to a local restaurant. The queue's progress was continually interrupted by the receptionist feeling obliged to pause to answer the telephone, and so I decided to find the hotel's reception number and call her from my mobile. Not surprisingly she answered, and I began to ask my question, and as I did so made my way forward to the front of the queue, only to be met with a wave of the hand indicating that she was busy on the phone! It acted as a powerful illustration of how difficult it is to break patterned communications behaviour.

## It's Not Big Brother

In the introduction of collaborative working, as we shall see later, there are both advantages and some attendant drawbacks. Whilst in my experience the drawbacks are relatively minor and can be controlled or mitigated, as with any major programme of change, individuals naturally focus on the negative issues first (a form of self-protection) and are often unable to let go of the perceived disadvantages and move forward, but instead dwell on, worry and fret about the negative consequences. This prevents them from moving on to consider and appreciate the major and more significant advantages of collaborative working.

One of the major issues which often arises is the introduction of cameras. They are an integral part of visual collaboration, yet people often view them negatively, feel they are somewhat intrusive, that they are being constantly watched, and see them as 'Big Brother'.

This is something we will consider in more detail later when we look at how collaborative change programmes can be designed and implemented.

## Don't Marginalise Negativity

Again, something we will discuss later, in the section on managing change, is that any perceived disadvantages must not be marginalised or ignored, but must be taken seriously. Although they could appear relatively small in comparison to the obvious commercial advantages, they need to be discussed, debated and considered so their relevance can be seen in perspective and allowed to naturally dissipate.

There can, however, be occasions when the negativity is completely inappropriate, as was borne out in one collaboration assignment I was leading, which involved connecting a remote production facility with a head office support function. The head of the support function dwelt on the negative ramifications of providing collaborative connectivity, stating that it would reduce face-to-face contact, hence damaging personal relationships and leading to production inefficiencies; he was not at all swayed by the positive benefits, which were:

- a reduction in travelling time
- savings in travel costs
- immediate access to technical expertise
- the ability to share technical data.

What transpired was that the real reason for his resistance was a personal and inappropriate relationship which he was having with someone at the remote site – something he wanted to protect and sustain. Of course, he was unable to use this in support of his rationale, so had to revert to articulating spurious disadvantages.

## Corporate Versus Personal Benefits

Another issue to consider when dealing with the benefits of any transformation or change programme is the distinction between corporate and personal benefits, and collaboration is no exception. Clearly, in some cases these could well coincide, and this will to a large extent depend upon what drives and motivates individuals, and their allegiance to and relationship with the company. What is evident is that any individual involved with or affected by the changes needs to receive tangible personal benefits from the implementation of the changes proposed in order to become and remain supportive. In collaboration, these personal advantages could include:

- wanting to be associated with progress
- the opportunity for personal learning
- provision of skills that support career progression
- the chance to 'showcase' their skills
- the opportunity to associate with new groups and people.

On the other hand, the personal disadvantages of collaboration might be:

- the effort required to acquire new skills
- having existing ways of working challenged
- being judged by other groups
- potentially increased workload
- the installation of visualisation, which could be perceived as intrusive.

Many companies, when confronted by personal objections, counter them with reference to the commercial benefits the proposed changes will bring to the organisation. Yet, even if these claims may be true, this only serves to belittle the sense of personal disadvantage which is real to the objector. Although these concerns may appear trivial to the senior management and the wider organisation, they still need to be listened to and dealt with. If the weight and strength of the counterarguments to someone's sense of personal disadvantage are so compelling that they appear to make the person's objections seem trivial, it might only encourage the objector to remain silent, leading to personal resentment, which will probably manifest itself in resistance to the implementation of the wider programme.

What is required is the time to debate and reflect on the advantages and disadvantages in a neutral and non-pressurised environment, so that individuals can realise that what they perceive to be negative consequences are in effect overshadowed and outweighed by the attendant advantages.

So, for example, being judged by other groups can provide a new perspective offering opportunities to facilitate more efficient, effective and even easier ways of working. The atmosphere in which the judgement is delivered needs to be one which is conducive to being seen as a form of constructive questioning rather than critical interrogation. This is particularly pertinent and relevant to collaborative working, where the disparate parties will want to protect the values and opinions that help to bond each group together.

This is something we will deal with in more detail when we look at how to design, implement and manage a collaborative change programme.

## Enabling Benefits

As we have mentioned already, collaboration provides individuals, and indeed the organisation, with a new capability. This capability itself can be seen as having no intrinsic value, because it is only when successfully applied that it provides organisational or commercial benefit.

Another way to look at it is that any capability is an 'enabler', and its true benefit will only be realised once it is applied in a real situation. For example, in assessing the benefit of expenditure incurred to educate a child privately, the value might only become apparent at a later date, as the child might have gained sufficient confidence and personal skills to perform more effectively at a job interview, and hence secure a foot on the career ladder. This is not intended as a political statement – just an example.

As another example, being courteous and polite might not be seen as having any immediate return, but it creates relationships and an atmosphere that enable effective, efficient and harmonious working and the attainment of both individual and mutual personal and corporate benefits.

The same is true of the corporate environment, where it is difficult to quantify the benefits of good working conditions, breakout areas, good-quality corporate catering and corporate socials; but they undoubtedly not only ensure that individuals feel they are well treated and make them feel positively disposed towards the organisation, but also encourage them to return the goodwill by being conscientious, diligent and productive in the application of their skills. It is even more important to deal with people issues in a collaborative change programme, as by definition there are more opportunities for interpersonal tension and conflicts in the situations that such a programme generates.

I am reminded of an occasion when I was helping to install a new collaborative environment in an organisation where the Operations Manager felt that dealing with people issues was unnecessary and said, "I employ people to come into work and I expect them to work, and I don't feel it necessary to deal with their personal well-being". The result was that, although the collaborative environment was installed and made operational, and although the technology was effective, personal disputes erupted on an ever-increasing basis, leading to a reduction in performance and efficiency.

When introducing collaboration into any organisation, if the senior management team tries to quantify the enabling benefits it affords in a traditional fashion and want hard, quantifiable, commercial data, there will undoubtedly be a severe problem! If the leaders 'just don't get it' because they are looking at the end result through the traditional cost–benefit lens, there will always be an uphill struggle, which will probably end in the collaborative programme stalling or being cancelled and the original sponsor being seen as the initiator of 'kite flying'!

In trying to persuade a traditionally-minded team leader who is biased towards facts and figures to spend capital resources, it will probably be damaging for a collaboration sponsor to talk about the benefits that will arise from creating a one-team feel or a united allegiance, or from providing the opportunity to receive positive reinforcement. Although these are all undoubtedly powerful enablers for any team wanting to achieve exceptional performance, their effects are not only difficult but virtually impossible to quantify!

What often happens in practice is that the justification paper will simply claim that the introduction of collaboration will yield a 1.5% increase in operational efficiency and a 2% reduction in operational costs – figures just plucked out of the air in the hope that they will not be questioned, but taken at face value. There will be numerous other proposals containing similar claims. What the company's senior leaders have to decide is which measures to support and which will have the most chances of delivering the claimed benefits.

This clamouring for access to finite funds to support competing projects was exemplified in one company I was involved with, where the CEO of a large manufacturing organisation said that, if he found money to support every project proposal, the aggregated cost-saving gains would enable him to produce the product for free!

## Benefits Quantification

The introduction of collaborative working will undoubtedly bring with it associated capital and revenue costs – capital costs to design and install the necessary hardware and software to effect the audio, visual and data connectivity, and revenue costs to provide the necessary training and coaching support. These costs will need to be offset by the potential but realistic attainment of future benefits, be they increases in productivity or a possible reduction in long-term revenue costs through the sharing of scarce resources.

However, as we have already discussed, since collaboration is a new capability and its benefits are tangential, it is difficult, and sometimes impossible, to actually quantify in precise terms its financial rewards. Given that expenditure cannot wholly be based upon an act of faith, there will need to be an element of "we need this capability", and for it to be seen as a natural progression in the communications process. After all, no company expects a team to justify the provision of mobile phones – they are just seen as a necessity! Collaboration must likewise become a natural and integral component of business practice.

That said, given below are a number of corporate and personal benefits and disadvantages that I have encountered when introducing collaborative working.

| BENEFITS | |
|---|---|
| CORPORATE | PERSONAL |
| Access to scarce expertise | Fewer interruptions |
| Ability to share learnings | Ability to showcase skills |
| Collective decision-making | More influence |
| Remote monitoring of equipment | More personal exposure |
| Fewer meetings and emails | Better employment opportunities |
| One-team feel | Association with success |

| DISADVANTAGES | |
|---|---|
| **CORPORATE** | **PERSONAL** |
| Group culture clash leading to conflicts | Feelings of loss of control |
| Confusion as to who is responsible for what | Sense of being second-guessed |
| Potential for 'stealing' people's time | Feelings of being monitored |
| Potential anarchy | Loss of autonomy |

This is something we will return to in some depth when we look at how to design and implement a collaborative change programme.

| KEY MESSAGES |
|---|
| • Collaboration is not a version of Big Brother |
| • Evaluate the advantages and disadvantages of collaborative working |
| • Remember to manage existing communication systems effectively so they don't disrupt an ongoing conversation or discussion |
| • Don't trivialise or marginalise negativity or objections by countering them with commercial advantages |
| • Don't appear to be critically judgemental of other groups' ways of working |
| • It is more critical to deal with people issues in collaborative working, as there are more opportunities for misunderstandings leading to personal conflict |
| • Don't try to use traditional cost–benefit analysis to justify collaboration |
| • Collaborative change must bring personal as well as corporate benefits |

# 3

## JOINING GROUPS TOGETHER

By definition, when collaborating you are joining groups together – groups that can interact together in real time and at any time.

The ability to interact in this way can clearly bring enormous benefits in improving operational efficiency and commercial performance. It can, however, also be fraught with sometimes unexpected complications around people issues that, if not surfaced and addressed, can lead to misunderstandings, confusion and on occasion personal and group conflicts; so, instead of collaboration resulting in performance improvements, it can potentially lead to efficiency losses.

### Organisational Culture

What we are trying to do is to form one combined and united team from two or more groups.

Each of these groups will have its own subculture, and will need to be joined to the other to form one cohesive team with one culture. However in joining groups together they may experience a form of 'culture clash', but before we move on to look at this in any more detail let's look at what we actually mean by 'organisational culture'. There are numerous definitions of culture, such as:

- It's the way we do things around here.
- It's a set of shared goals and values.
- It's the way the group acts, behaves and feels.
- It's the group's DNA.

All groups have a well-understood but unarticulated culture, and any new members joining the group will have to adhere to the expected ways of behaving, acting and thinking if they are to be accepted by other members of the group. Failure to adhere to these 'group norms' will result in the new group member being marginalised, ostracised, ignored, alienated, or eventually even being expelled from the group. Hence, whilst it is quite easy for individuals to physically join a group, new members will quickly have to assimilate to and understand the group norms and adhere to them, even to the extent where they may need to reverse some of their own views.

However, we are presented with an altogether more complex situation when we join two or more groups together. Different groups will undoubtedly have developed their own subcultures, and we therefore run the risk of misunderstandings developing, possibly leading to interpersonal conflict when we try to join them together. On many occasions I have seen groups joined in collaborative working which continue to view each other as 'enemies', and act to retain their own separate identities and ways of thinking.

## Culture Clash

The primary cause of any personal or group dissonance preventing effective collaboration is that the entities being joined together will undoubtedly have different, discrete cultures which, when brought together, can result in misunderstandings and misconceptions, and may even lead to interpersonal conflict – what can be termed 'culture clash'.

This culture clash can come as a total surprise, especially if the groups being joined are ostensibly 'on the same side', with explicitly stated similar primary objectives. Whilst it might be expected that two groups from different countries who need to work together may experience some communication and relationship issues, deriving from variations in their respective cultures, it may come as a surprise to find two internal groups within the same organisation experiencing some degree of interpersonal friction.

My own experience is that the wider the perceived differences between the cultures of the groups being joined together, the less likelihood there is of experiencing culture clash. Since the differences are more obvious, more account is taken of them, and actions are designed and implemented to mitigate them. This is probably because, if we know and see that there are cultural differences, we are more liable to make an effort to accommodate them, but when we think the cultures to be the same, we are more likely to presume that there will be no issues in joining the groups together. In addition, groups with different subcultures in the same organisation interacting on an infrequent basis might well make allowance for and accept differences in style, behaviour and attitudes, but since collaboration provides the opportunity for continuous interaction, smaller differences can become magnified and act as stressors to fracture relationships.

Let's face it, how often have you been friends with someone whom you see on a regular basis and think you share the same personal culture, as you seem to get along so well, only to realise that when you spend a long period of time together, for example on an extended holiday, you are unable to live with the small differences and can't wait for the holiday to finish!

In collaboration, you are forcing people and groups together, and they will only become an effective team once they understand, accept and accommodate each other's point of view and accept their differences in thinking and behaving.

This culture clash can be particularly severe when companies move from an area-based structure, where individuals are fully supportive of improving the performance of a specific production entity, to a functional model, where production personnel are encouraged to interact with their functional colleagues on a more regular basis. The reality is that operational teams derive satisfaction from acting in real time, whereas functional teams are often more comfortable having time to gestate and reflect on issues, and these differences can on occasion cause severe culture clash and misinterpretation of the motives behind each other's behaviour and attitudes.

The operational team could view the functional team's desire to reflect as procrastination, whereas the functional team might see the operational team's immediacy as a knee-jerk reaction.

## Values Drive Culture

One useful way of looking at culture is to define what underpins its formation and sustains its identity. In essence, it is what each individual values that will bond the group together and define how people act and behave towards each other, and will also determine the group's beliefs, attitudes and accepted behaviours.

For example, the primary collective value of a group of social drinkers in a local pub might be free-flowing conversations where ideas are proffered without fear of them being ridiculed, instead acting as triggers to promote wide-ranging, exploratory and often amusing and entertaining conversations. In the pub group culture no one is trying to find out the truth based on facts; group members are merely immersing themselves in a situation where they behave to sustain the value of harmless banter. To cut short this banter by stating an indisputable truth would be to act against the group's value set, and the perpetrator would soon be marginalised and left sitting in the corner of the pub with few friends, labelled as the 'pub bore'!

Whilst this social group example might seem somewhat trivial, the principle is equally valid in work groups, where accepted values, often unarticulated, bond the group together and need to be recognised by others joining the group. Sometimes it is necessary for individuals to sacrifice some level of their own personal values in order to satisfy the values of the organisation or team they belong to. If they hide personal values which are eventually exposed – and they will be – they will be seen as deceitful, and their influence in the team marginalised.

As an example, individuals might place a higher value on some of the following personal factors than on the performance of the team itself:

- career
- opinions
- power and authority
- influence
- status.

In joining groups together it is imperative that the combined team shares the same values. Clearly, in a production setting the primary value of the combined team should be related to performance. Subgroups might have their own discrete and desirable individual values – for example, a highly technical team would value acquiring knowledge in their discipline, but this should not be at the expense of ensuring that this knowledge is only applied if it improves performance for the wider team.

The major cause of conflict, not only in business but in every other aspect of life, is when two individuals or groups are interacting but are driven by different values. For example, in family life a teenager might value leisure activities and socialisation, whereas the parents might put a higher value on their education, resulting in continual tension in the prioritisation of activities, leading to friction between them.

In an industrial setting I have also seen interpersonal conflict in heavily unionised organisations where the manager and shop steward both have the same values, that of power and influence, which is inappropriate because their joint value should be the success of the organisation. However, this may mean one or both of them relinquishing some power.

On occasion, it is worth encouraging people to ask themselves what they actually value, which might provoke them to articulate what they feel they ought to value rather than what they actually do. In seminars people always quote health as one of their core values, whereas in deeper discussion it is evident that their lifestyle does little to nurture it.

## Competing Values

One issue that needs to be raised is that of individual competing values. One person might value honesty, but be sufficiently sensitive not to be too honest so as to hurt someone's feelings when providing them with feedback on their own behaviour. Here we have the competing values of honesty and sensitivity.

Another social example would be an individual who values honesty and also friendship; so, if at a casino this person were to observe a friend 'cheating', does he or she expose this to the casino to satisfy the honesty value, or simply have a quiet word with the friend later? An extreme example, but one which hopefully illustrates the point.

## Group Beliefs and Norms

What a group values is often articulated in the form of a series of accepted beliefs or norms, which might range from another group being seen as inherently lazy, ineffective and incompetent, to the company itself being deemed unfair. Any new person joining the group might well challenge these strongly held beliefs and so risk causing group disharmony. It is these beliefs that bond the group together and often provide it with its identity and sense of belonging. The perceived truth of these beliefs is reinforced by a form of 'perceptual defence', where group members only allow information to enter the group that reinforces and sustains its original set of beliefs.

In fact, on most occasions there will be one or two individuals within the group who act to 'police' the norms and ensure they are maintained. This can, however, cause confusion when trying to gauge the mood of a group by holding individual conversations

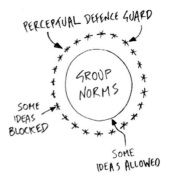

where these enforcers are not present. In one-to-one conversations the output can appear very positive, whereas when the same questions are asked in a group setting where the enforcers are present the responses can be completely opposite and often negative. Interestingly, these individuals are often not the official designated leaders of teams, but emerge as unofficial intermediaries, influencers and opinion-formers.

For example, a leader might be characterised by the group as ineffective. New members joining the group will have to be seen to reinforce this view by overtly providing anecdotal evidence of negative actions, behaviours and traits which support it.

When interacting with a new company I am often confronted with a situation where a particular individual is cast as 'difficult', awkward and negative, but I then find that there is no evidence to support the charges; instead, it has just become a group norm which provides team members with an easily identifiable adversary.

This can apply to any group: how often have we heard an operational team cast aspersions on the competence of a well-intended support function? All too often the HR or IT functions are soft and easy targets. These strong yet often ill-informed beliefs about the competence of other groups could be borne out of the desire to create a common and easily identifiable 'enemy'.

In collaboration the key requirement is to ensure that the enemy is outside of the combined collaborative team, which could mean competitors in the marketplace or indeed simply poor performance.

In the design and implementation of collaborative working, I have seen groups holding negative perceptions of each other gradually having to reassess, revalue and even reverse these views when they interact in real time on a continuous basis. This reversal is by no means easy, as an individual or group might need to challenge the 'investment' made in arriving at an ingrained view, and in some cases sacrificing this could be a painful and difficult process.

## Individual Attitudes and Behaviours

A group's values and beliefs give rise to individuals' attitudes and behaviours. The attitudes and behaviours an individual exhibits are a choice, but will be encouraged by the overarching accepted, but not necessarily explicitly espoused, values of the group itself. So, if the group values harmony, and believes harmony will improve performance, individuals will tend to adopt a style that promotes strong personal bonds, and will be able to work supportively to achieve a common objective. Anyone can choose to be positive or negative, critical or helpful, supportive or oppositional.

In one workshop, when I was talking about positivity and negativity and explaining that there is always a positive to every negative, as it is a choice, one individual who had been consistently negative throughout the day asked: "What is positive about me being here listening to your rubbish?" Clearly I wasn't going down too well with this individual, but I risked pointing out to him that the positive of him being at the workshop listening to me was that the 20 or so people he normally interacted with at work had at least had a day off from suffering from his unremitting negativity!

It is also important to distinguish between a personal quality and an individual's attitudes and behaviours. A personal quality is an inherent trait, and is more difficult, if not impossible, to modify or significantly change. For example, an individual could be naturally creative, which is an inherent gift, but have a choice as to how to use this 'talent' – in other words, in their attitude or behaviour. Some people will opt to use this creativity to put obstacles in the way of good ideas in order to delay, defer or even prevent them from being implemented, or indeed might use their creativity to be cynical and negative, whereas other people might use their creativity to develop options or enhance somebody else's ideas.

The choice of behaviour is not to be confused with business skills, and I have often found that individuals with exceptionally poor attitudes, who create poor morale within the wider team, are at pains to reference their immense business acumen, experience and skill so as to counter the negative effects of their behaviour on the wider team.

My own view is that no matter how potentially useful a person's skill set is, be it welding, bookkeeping or business analysis, if someone upsets, demotivates or otherwise depresses 20 other people at work, that person might do the business a favour and stay at home!

Probably two of the most powerful learnings that I have gained about behaviour are:

- Behaviour is contagious, so if a person is energetic and optimistic this can infect the wider team, whereas if they are downbeat and depressive this can bring the team's energy and morale down.
- Behaviour is a reaction to the way you are treated, and so if someone treats you with fairness and respect, you will return this by being cooperative, whereas if they act aggressively you might feel the need to retaliate as a form of redress.

## The Behavioural Sliding Scale

Behaviour lies on a scale along which individuals will move up and down depending upon their personality and the reaction of the person they are interacting with. To provide an example, such an interactive sliding style scale could range from:

ENTHUSIASTIC ➡ FORTHRIGHT ➡ DOMINANT ➡ AGGRESSIVE ➡ BULLYING

The real danger is that someone might initially be forthright in his or her views, but, if the recipient reacts in an intransigent way, in order to get the point across the initiator gradually, but unknowingly, slides along the scale, and his or her behaviour might then be perceived by the recipient as aggressive or even bullying.

## Style and Impact Reviews

The traditional methodology used to help individuals gain an understanding of how their style is received and perceived by others is to carry out a 360° exercise, whereby their manager, peers and direct reports provide feedback via a questionnaire. The output is usually provided in the form of a series of graphs and spider diagrams, and whilst this provides some indication of how their behaviour affects others, it is somewhat limiting and one-dimensional, and doesn't provide the opportunity for issues to be explored in more detail and the underlying reasons for their behaviour to be identified.

It is more effective, insightful and useful to carry out a style and impact review and gain inputs from a variety of people with whom the individual interacts on a regular basis via confidential, one-to-one conversations. These conversations provide the opportunity to draw out emerging themes, explore issues in more depth and gain a more accurate and detailed view of how the individual's style impacts on others. Narrative feedback is produced and can be used as the basis for further confidential, reflective conversations that enable the individual to identify whether any modifications to their own personal style might help them to be more effective.

The power of this technique was demonstrated to me in one style and impact review I carried out, where it gradually emerged that the individual had a tendency to over-talk in meetings; he felt this added value, but in fact it had the reverse effect and his domineering approach prevented useful dialogue which would have led to better decisions.

In the feedback I mentioned this to him, which elicited the response, "I totally disagree", and he estimated that he only talked at meetings for 10% of the time. I left that point and moved on to other aspects of his style. Two weeks later he stopped me in a corridor and apologised and said that he now realised that he did talk for most of the time at meetings, but hadn't realised it before!

In another example it was clear that people feared the person concerned, as he used his intellect to interrogate everyone's ideas, views and opinions, which people found uncomfortable at best and bullying at worst. It even extended to people leaving the office via a roundabout route to avoid passing his room. Although the office door was left open, they perceived that being called into it was akin to being trapped in a spider's web.

In the feedback discussion we moved on to the topic of his interrogatory style, which he felt was advantageous in seeking a deeper understanding of people's motives and a way of encouraging them to act to solve existing problems; but he was clearly blissfully unaware that it was threatening and made people feel very uncomfortable and therefore had the effect of marginalising him from ad hoc conversations.

## Group Culture

A useful way of depicting any group's culture is by reference to the group's values and beliefs and individuals' attitudes and behaviours. We can depict this in the form of a 'culture box', within which we are able to freely move around safely, comfortably sharing views, ideas and thoughts, secure in the knowledge that any espoused ideas and opinions will be accepted by others, hence keeping the group bonded together.

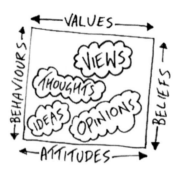

Problems arise when the culture boxes of two groups joined together by collaboration do not fit neatly over each other and there is some form of misalignment. This has the potential to generate personal confusion and disharmony from this cultural misalignment which is shown below:

OPPORTUNITIES FOR
MISUNDERSTANDING .

As discussed earlier, what is required is to agree a new set of values, attitudes and behaviours which will create one culture box and bond the two groups together to form one cohesive team.

## The Cogs of Culture

Another way of depicting the culture of an organisation is as a series of interconnecting cogs which mesh together and drive processes, procedures and actions. The 'value cog' will be the largest and most influential, but is also the most easy to disguise.

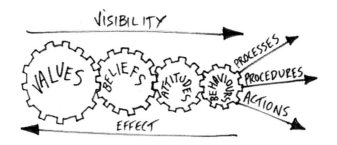

This means that individuals can hide what they really value, for example their career aspirations, and act and behave to support this value, perhaps by promoting themselves to more senior management, even though their overtly stated value is group performance; others therefore become confused by their outward visible behaviour.

Yet another way of depicting organisational culture is to liken it to a tree, as shown below, where the values are the roots, but are hidden; the beliefs are the trunk that supports the branches, representing the attitudes, and which are flexible; and finally, the fruit of the tree represents the resultant behaviour, which is the outcome.

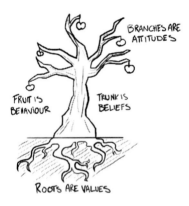

To extend this analogy, in order to improve the crop it is more effective to fertilise and water the roots rather than pay attention to other parts of the tree!

It is also true to say that, if an individual's values are shallow, the tree will be easily uprooted by any significant winds of change.

## Espoused Versus Actual Values

Most organisational leaders spend an enormous amount of time and resources defining the core values that they would like to believe underpin the culture of the organisation, and often display them in prominent positions within the company. These values are rolled out to the workforce, pinned on noticeboards, given to individuals on laminated cards, fanfared at 'town hall' meetings, and discussed in team meetings and focus groups.

Unfortunately, in my experience, whilst these are the espoused values which the company would like to exemplify, in reality the organisation often works to a different set of actual values, and this can cause deep resentment in the workforce; individuals will often then respond by acting negatively and critically, and even showing hostility towards the company and the leaders themselves.

It is essential that, if the values are to be prominently displayed, the leaders must ensure that they themselves act in a way that overtly supports them, so that they are seen as respected role models.

Also, the company must be mature and honest enough to articulate and display the values it actually wants. It is too easy for the company to cite the corporate core values as:

- respect
- teamwork
- freedom
- integrity.

Whilst on most occasions these might be desirable and laudable, what the company really values over everything is:

- profit
- shareholder value
- cash flow
- volume growth.

Being honest about stating the latter will mean that any actions regarding cost reductions, including shedding staff, will be easier to defend and explain.

> These double standards were demonstrated in one assignment in which one of the company's core values was stated as "Freedom to Act", whereas in reality in every aspect of corporate life the company exhibited a severe restriction on individuals' views and actions supported by an authoritarian management style.

## Joining Different Countries' Cultures Together

The literature is awash with material on the cultural differences between countries. These differences can be described in various ways, but the majority always contain topics such as:

### Decision-making

People from some cultures prefer to take more individual decisions, whereas others prefer to confer and establish consensus. I have often found at syndicate sessions that, if you ask a UK group for an answer to a question, individuals will openly shout out their answers, whereas those from African and Asian countries will confer between themselves to arrive at a group answer as they feel more comfortable with consensus.

## Risk

Some cultures have a natural tendency to be risk averse, whereas members of others are happy taking what they perceive to be calculated risks.

## Hierarchy

The major difference here is that some cultures are more comfortable with a strong, well-defined hierarchy and are less comfortable in discussions at a higher level in the organisation, whilst some prefer 'flatter' or less hierarchical organisations which facilitate open conversations with anyone within the organisation.

## Leadership Style

Some cultures encourage a more dominant and even aggressive leadership style, whereas others prefer one based on empathy and compassion.

Joining cultures together when they exhibit these different traits produces a new level of complexity in collaborative working: one which needs to be taken into consideration when building a united team.

Further practical examples of topics that I have found need to be taken into consideration are given below.

## Speech Patterns

I was working in one collaborative environment where the European team was connected with a group from

Asia. The speech style of the European group was to allow and even encourage individuals  to talk over the initial speaker, so gaining control of the conversation. This process was completely seamless and was not seen as rude. Unfortunately, the Asian team's style was to prefer to allow someone to finish speaking and pause slightly, and then someone else would speak; to interrupt someone was seen as discourteous. This meant that on many occasions the Asian group members rarely spoke, as there was no suitable gap to enable them to enter the conversation.

## Inappropriate Jokes

I have seen many British people tell a joke which included a reference to a family member (not necessarily by name). For example, there might be a typical mother-in-law joke, which is sometimes accepted as humorous and non-offensive in British culture, but seen as highly disrespectful in countries where the family unit is sacrosanct.

## Stance

Whilst engaging in casual or relaxed conversation, Europeans often recline and put their feet on a chair or desk, exposing the soles of their feet – an insult in many other cultures.

Also, every culture has a determined but undefined sense of personal space which separates them when they have a face-to-face conversation. If this sense of space is different between members of two cultures it can result in an almost comical situation, with the individual who requires less space almost chasing the person who requires more space around the room!

## Language

Clearly it is imperative to understand and accept that, if people from one country are conversing in a language other than their mother tongue, it is necessary to take this into account and allow them extra time to express themselves, and also take cognisance of the fact that some of their phraseology may unintentionally be confusing.

Interestingly, I was working for a UK company in a production operation overseas where the English-speaking control room staff had to pass instructions via a radio system to local operational engineers on site who had learned English on intensive language courses. On one occasion, the native English-speaking ex-pat operator passed an instruction to his non-native English-speaking colleague. The instruction was: "Can you open the P101 valve?" The response from the local national engineer was: "Yes." The control room operator waited for the valve to open, but there was no action, so he reiterated the instruction with slightly stronger emphasis, but still to no effect. At the third time of asking he shouted to the external operator: "Can you open the ***** valve?" The surprised and hesitant response was: "Yes, I can. When do you want me to do it?" The local engineer's English was so 'good' that for him "can you" meant "are you capable of opening it?", whereas "will you" was an instruction.

## Mergers and Acquisitions

A critical activity that often pays no attention to organisational culture is the area of mergers and acquisitions. The acquiring company could well have a completely different culture to the one it is either acquiring or merging with, which could lead to misunderstandings and possible interpersonal friction, leading to reductions in efficiencies.

I have seen billion-dollar-turnover companies acquiring smaller operations concentrate their integration activities on simply ensuring the acquired company understands and adheres to the existing organisation's processes and procedures and taking no time to understand the cultural differences.

What is required is to map out the two cultures and understand how the differences will affect full and effective integration.

| KEY MESSAGES |
|---|
| • Culture is "the way we do things around here" |
| • Joining two groups together, each having their own subculture, can cause 'culture clash' |
| • What groups value underpins their culture |
| • Don't use perceptual defence to justify your existing views and opinions |
| • Behaviour is a choice |
| • Don't try to excuse bad behaviour by reference to strong business skills |
| • Behaviour is contagious |
| • Individuals react to the way they are treated |
| • Consider the application of style and impact reviews to augment the traditional 360° process |

| |
|---|
| • Ask yourself the question: what do you really value? |
| • Are the espoused values of the company the ones that the company actually exhibits? |
| • Beware of competing values |
| • Identify the enforcers of the group's norms |
| • Ensure the 'enemy' is outside of the groups being joined together |
| • A personal quality can be used either positively or negatively |

# 4

## CHANGING CULTURE

Through collaboration we are joining two cultures together to produce a new one, and therefore the groups being joined together must agree their joint values to produce the new culture. I have been asked many times how long it takes to change an organisation's culture, and my stock answer is that it depends on the strength of the drivers.

A vivid example to illustrate this point is of the rugby team that crashed in the Andes in 1972. With no rescuers arriving for several months, and with several dead, the survivors decided it was necessary to eat those who had died in order to survive. If they had been asked before they boarded the plane if one of their values was cannibalism, the answer would undoubtedly have been a short, sharp and direct "No", but, given the need to survive, their collective values changed.

This is, of course, a highly exaggerated example of culture change, but it serves to illustrate the power of drivers and how they can act as powerful motivators to facilitate change.

We will be examining how to plan, develop and implement a suitable change programme to produce a united culture in the next chapter, but firstly it is imperative that we understand the cultures of the groups being joined together, which can be ascertained by carrying out a culture review.

## Culture Reviews

Once cultures are understood, actions and initiatives can be introduced to produce the new desired culture that will support the attainment of jointly agreed standards and targets. However, assessing, understanding, defining and articulating the nature of existing cultures is fraught with difficulty, as people are often reticent to voice what they really feel and value, as these beliefs may run counter to accepted company norms.

An attempt to understand and reveal the culture via traditional questionnaires all too often produces a one-dimensional and distorted view. In order to genuinely understand any culture the information needs to be collected via:

- confidential one-to-one discussions
- attendance at group meetings
- observations of people at work
- sensing and feeling the prevailing atmosphere.

In one-to-one discussions it is important to draw out and gradually deepen themes to understand what bonds the group together and where allegiances lie, and what the individual and team drivers are. It is also imperative to gradually drill down in a non-threatening way, and bring to the surface the true reasons why people behave and think as they do, rather than accepting the first articulated response.

So, for example, an early question might be about what communication is like, which may elicit the traditional response of "It's inadequate". Rather than leaving it there, supplementary questions can help to gain a deeper understanding of the culture, such as:

- What would you like to know?
- Why haven't you asked anyone for information about it?
- Do you feel your questions will be answered truthfully and honestly?
- Have your own or someone else's questions ever been trivialised?

The collective responses to these questions should clearly provide a deeper understanding of the actual culture within the organisation. If an individual feels unable to ask questions through fear of receiving a negative or hostile response, this may be a consequence of an overly aggressive leadership style resulting in deferential acquiescence.

Also, when carrying out the culture review, every aspect of the way the review is accepted, and the way people react to it, is a critical input for understanding and defining the actual culture. For example, as has happened to me on numerous occasions, if you receive curt and almost rude responses to requests for individual discussions, interestingly this in itself could be an indication of:

- a feeling of distrust in the process
- a sense that there is an alternative and more sinister reason why the review has been initiated
- a genuine work overload created by an overly demanding leadership style
- a distrust of any external input.

In one assignment I was carrying out for a telecommunications organisation, I received a very poor response to my request for one-to-one discussions. I casually mentioned this to my sponsoring client, who immediately and without my knowledge sent an email to all staff instructing them to give me as much time as I needed. This one act told me more about the culture than the conversations that followed!

An alternative scenario I have often witnessed is where individuals are all too keen to talk, in a desire to publicly acknowledge how well they are treated and how proud they are to work for the organisation.

## Beware of your Culture Goggles!

In reviewing your own culture it is imperative that you are aware that you are carrying out any evaluation through your own culture goggles. If your lenses are red, the world is red, and only when you take them off can you see the true colours. So, if you perceive the organisation as unfair, it will remain unfair through your lenses.

It is therefore very difficult for an organisation to evaluate its own culture. Without wishing to appear to promote the use of external consultants, it does require the review to be undertaken by somebody who is totally neutral. In fact, if the organisation has an aggressive, over-demanding culture, the review itself will be carried out through this culture, which will simply encourage acquiescence and fail to identify the true culture.

The external resource chosen to carry out a culture review has to be sufficiently confident and robust to provide the feedback in a forthright, honest, yet respectful way. This might, on occasion, not be what the senior leadership team wants to hear, and hence the consultant runs the risk of receiving no further assignments from the company, or maybe even having the assignment's value and associated costs challenged – a further insight into the company's culture!

In one culture review I carried out it emerged that the underlying culture was one of malicious compliance brought about by an overly aggressive and demanding management style. On receiving this feedback, the executive leadership team verbally attacked me for over half an hour, until I halted the onslaught by suggesting they were using their aggressive style to attempt to cast aspersions on the output from the study – which was precisely the behaviour that had generated the culture that the review had defined!

On another occasion it was clear that the organisational culture was controlling, confrontational and suspicious, something that was reinforced and overtly demonstrated when I suggested how the culture might be modified and the HR director accused me of simply seeking further work – a clear example not only of his own deep suspicion, but how he was viewing my motives through his own value system.

In another assignment, for a company which had a nationwide fleet of delivery vehicles, a culture review had been initiated to find out why staff morale was very low. In carrying out the exercise it was necessary to spend many days with the delivery drivers, and it soon became apparent that the overarching culture was one of resentment as a result of the application of internal processes which were perceived as based on double standards. The workforce saw them as inherently unfair, which resulted in resentment directed towards the company, low morale and poor quality of work. The individual examples of these perceived double standards in practice might seem quite trivial, but they clearly had an enormous effect on the mindset and attitudes of the staff. For example, delivery drivers had to buy their own maps in order to find customers, whereas supervisors and managers were provided with Sat Nav systems so they could locate the drivers with ease. Also, in the event of an accident, delivery drivers had to pay the £500 insurance excess, in an attempt by the company to promote careful driving – again, something not imposed on management.

The output from a culture review should not necessarily be complex; it can be described simply, in a few sentences, and can be used to feed into more wide-ranging group workshops and activities to decide whether the current culture supports the attainment of group and corporate objectives. It can also be used in the design of a programme of change to move the organisation towards the desired culture.

## The Danger of Questionnaires!

As mentioned earlier, some organisations and companies prefer to carry out exercises to understand the existing culture by use of questionnaires completed by individual members of the organisation. This is an inadequate way of assessing and defining organisational culture for the following reasons:

- Only those who are interested in the exercise will complete the survey.
- It is difficult to ask supplementary questions to gain a deeper understanding of why people think as they do.
- No matter how strong the reassurances provided, there is a reluctance to put delicate views concerning emotions, feelings and personal thoughts into writing.
- Many people think the company will take no action and so won't bother to fill the questionnaire in; these people could be the opinion-formers who sustain the existing culture.

The main reason why management teams often revert to the use of questionnaires is that it is a relatively simple way of collecting and displaying views, but there are fundamental flaws. For example, if we take the category of communication (always included in any culture survey), and if each category has a ranking of 1 to 20, with 20 being good and 1 being bad, let's say that in a given year the result for communication is a score of 5, with 30% of the population completing the questionnaire. If it is then repeated the following year and the score is 4 with a 70% completion rate, this could be used to demonstrate an improvement in communication!

The reason is that 40% more people have now bothered to complete the questionnaire, leading to the reasonable assumption that their earlier apathy has now turned into interest. Had they completed the questionnaire the first year, the result might well have been only 2!

As can be seen from this example, reliance on questionnaires might provide the leadership team with a false view of what the majority of people think, as they only assess a small population of potentially more positively orientated individuals. This could result in the wrong issues being identified, and therefore wrong actions being developed to solve them, leaving the real issues unattended, and providing ammunition for detractors to reinforce their negative view that these issues are not being tackled.

I am not saying that questionnaires do not have a part to play – they can be an input – but they can be misleading when trying to understand relationships, emotions and feelings. They need to be supplemented with face-to-face, private and confidential discussions, along with sensing the prevailing atmosphere.

If a company does insist on using a questionnaire, one of the suggestions I make (which is sometimes unfortunately not taken up) is to end the questionnaire with two insightful questions:

- Would you like the management to take notice of this survey?
- Do you think they will?

The answers can be very illuminating!

| KEY MESSAGES AND QUESTIONS |
|---|
| • Periodically review your existing culture |
| • If you are changing the culture, what are the key drivers, and are they sufficiently strong to facilitate the change? |
| • Don't rely on questionnaires for understanding the existing culture |
| • Be careful that you aren't seeing the world through your own 'Culture Goggles' |

# 5

## MANAGING COLLABORATIVE CHANGE PROGRAMMES

Having defined the required culture and evaluated the existing subcultures of the groups being joined together, the organisation can move on to planning, designing and implementing an appropriate change programme.

Most companies will be familiar with, and experienced in, traditional change management theory and practice; however, there are subtle differences when designing a collaborative change programme, and some of these issues are discussed in this chapter.

### New Capability

As already mentioned, the ability to collaborate is a capability, and as such its implementation needs to be managed differently to a conventional change programme.

Most change programmes can be categorised into four main types:

- process
- technology
- organisational
- capability.

Introducing a new process change requires the necessary and appropriate training, without which it would be impossible to adopt new or amended systems and procedures. For example, the installation of a new control system would necessitate an operator receiving the appropriate rigorous training in how to use it to ensure the new functionality is utilised to maximise performance.

A similar situation exists with technologically-driven change or transformation programmes. For example, the introduction of a new telephone system simply requires effective training in how to use the technology.

Further, organisational change programmes require the redesign of business processes, and a review of individual roles and responsibilities.

However, when introducing a capability transformation programme such as collaborative working, rather than the emphasis being on training, we instead need a bias towards education and awareness. The users themselves have to decide how the new capability might best be incorporated and utilised in order to modify existing ways of working, and hence achieve improvements in performance and efficiency.

## What is a Capability?

What do we actually mean by a new 'capability'? In essence, it is the provision of a new skill or competence that is acquired without any overt connection to actions, but which, if applied correctly, will yield a potential secondary advantage.

I am reminded of an assignment in the oil and gas industry when I was providing support to an organisation in the creation and use of a collaborative environment. One of the senior managers, who was clearly opposed to having his stable world disturbed by the new connectivity capability, rather tersely asked me to identify at least five advantages that would be gained from introducing collaboration. My tactful response was to explain that the collaborative capability would provide him with the opportunity to interact in real time with his support staff, and that it was up to him to decide how this new capability might be used to his own advantage. During the ensuing discussion I attempted to mellow his slightly aggressive approach by reference to a neutral example of a man who drove a car from A to B, and the journey took him four hours. Providing the man with a new car capable of travelling faster, but still safely, might save him two hours; yet it would not be up to me to decide how he might profitably utilise the time gained, as only he knew his work schedule and priorities. This did seem to pacify the manager, and enabled us to have a more rational conversation about how he could utilise his own new capability to improve production and commercial advantage.

## The Need for Education

As we have already seen, the introduction and implementation of a collaborative transformation programme requires a bias towards education and awareness, which can be provided by a combination of:

- awareness workshops
- facilitated discussions
- one-to-one conversations
- group discussions.

These activities provide time for the individuals who will be using this capability to gradually become familiar with the potential benefits it provides. This early opportunity for reflection and gestation is necessary to enable individuals to come to terms with any possible perceived negatives, and to understand and appreciate the potential power of incorporating the capability into developing new ways of working.

## Pace

Before we look at the programme itself, it is worth pointing out that, to deal effectively with people issues in any change programme, the pace at which you move from one phase to the next is critical. Unlike process or physical environment changes, where the programme can be planned and implemented against a rigid timescale with milestone targets, when dealing with people issues it is necessary to move on only when people have fully understood the concepts and associated benefits of each phase of the programme. The rate of progress will therefore depend upon people's acceptance, and to move too fast could create confusion, leading to misunderstandings and even resentment.

That said, there will be occasions when it is necessary to accelerate the programme, even when there are still some doubters, who will hopefully be turned into strong supporters as the group norm moves towards one of support.

The timing of when to move is dependent upon the strength and influence of the resisters, and a judgement about whether they might derail the programme at a later date. To dwell too long on dealing with unnecessary intransigence could be perceived as a sign of weakness, and hence have negative repercussions on the sponsors.

A useful analogy is to see the change plan as a train which starts off with everybody on board, fully committed and clearly all moving along in the same direction. As the train gathers speed there is a danger that some dissenters will move towards the rear coaches and then uncouple themselves, resulting in the train containing the leaders in the forward carriages moving even faster, but leaving a significant number of people behind whom they thought were still supporters!

## The Change Programme

Any change programme needs to move from making people (often referred to as 'targets' in the literature, although my own personal view is that this makes them seem more like unwilling victims!) aware of the need for, and benefits of, the implementation of the programme, and enable them to become fully supportive and eventually actively participate. Consideration therefore needs to be given to:

- gaining an understanding of the need for and benefits of collaborating

- providing the opportunity to acquire a new perspective
- gaining acceptance
- encouraging genuine involvement.

Let's take each phase in turn.

## Gaining Understanding

What is required here is the design of a communication plan that enables people to:

- gain an understanding of the purpose and benefits of collaboration
- recognise that collaboration is simply a natural progression in the communication process
- accept that it is not a threat
- appreciate the issues that might arise when joining groups with different cultures together
- understand there might be a need to modify individual values and behaviours
- accept the need to understand the views and ideas of other people.

## Acquiring Perspective

Individuals can exist quietly and effectively in their own work group for many years, if not their whole working life, without really having to accept or deal with the different views and behaviours of other groups and people. This insularity creates a sense of security, and will undoubtedly be enhanced by associating with other team members who hold similar attitudes and beliefs. By introducing collaboration, individuals will have their own views, assumptions and ways of working challenged by other groups, which could lead to discomfort, dissonance and even personal conflict. In effect, it asks people to take a different perspective on their ways of thinking and the business processes they have adopted; how easy this will be depends both on the individual's ability to change their perspective and how strong the 'group-think' is.

This new perspective can be acquired by one-to-one and group discussions that do not force people to think differently (a process which might only serve to deepen their current views) but simply provide them with alternatives which they can reflect on in order to reach a new perspective. Providing too robust a challenge at an early stage will cause people to become more entrenched in their views, which they may not be able to counter, and could make them feign agreement whilst still remaining negative.

A simple yet powerful illustration of how two groups can look at the same situation for many years without realising that their own perspective emanates directly from their particular line of sight would be to show two eyes viewing an object from different sides, one rough and one smooth, as shown below.

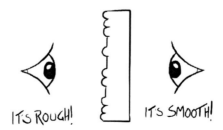

Asking for a description of the object would produce different accounts: rough, smooth, rough, smooth... Eventually the two viewers would come to realise that they were describing the same object, but from different perspectives – but only if they took the time and expended the energy to move around and view the object from the other's perspective.

## Gaining Acceptance and Dealing with "Yes, but..."

Having understood the need for and benefits of collaboration, and gained an understanding of a different group's perspective, we can then move on to gaining acceptance of the programme itself.

Here it is important to distinguish between acceptance of the benefits of the concepts of collaboration and the detailed implementation of the programme itself. It is critical to get people to park (and I mean park, not crush) any concerns they may have, indicating to them that their concerns will be addressed as part of the change programme, but gain their agreement that the concept itself is a good idea in principle. This is something we will deal with in more detail later, but in introducing any new concept, particularly involving interactions between people, it is normal for individuals to raise potential negative consequences for them personally – a natural form of survival.

It is akin to asking someone to work overseas, receiving responses such as: "Will I be accompanied?", "Will I receive a tax-free allowance?", "How many trips home will I have a year?" Whilst these are all perfectly valid questions, the answer to the primary concept is: "Do you want to work overseas, yes or no?". If they say yes you can then move on to discussing the detail around benefits, working conditions, remuneration, etc.

## Encouraging Involvement

Involving people at every stage of the change programme is critical, helping them to remain positive, and ensuring that the programme becomes fully and irreversibly embedded in the new organisation. This helps to produce not only immediate and tangible commercial benefits, but also a more appropriate and self-sustaining organisational culture.

The important element in this involvement is that it must be genuine, and not manufactured or contrived. Natural and genuine involvement generates open and supportive attitudes, whereas contrived involvement will eventually be perceived as deceitful, and will only serve to make people feel cheated, causing them to become distant and even hostile to the programme.

> The importance of involvement in shaping behaviour was illustrated to me quite surprisingly by a prison governor (whom I was visiting as a business colleague rather than a 'guest'!) who said the prison service had realised that prisoners' behaviour was positively modified if they were given the opportunity to become involved in 'minor' decisions that affected their daily routine. This was prefaced by the governor referencing the fact that the prison service had recognised some time ago that the prisoners themselves had two advantages over the guards – there were more of them, and they were usually physically stronger – and therefore treating them with respect was a way of ensuring they were easier to manage.

## The Plan

The plan required to design and implement a collaborative change programme will contain all the necessary traditional initiatives required to gain and sustain active support from stakeholders, although, as mentioned earlier, there will need to be more time, effort and resources expended at the front end of the programme so that everyone understands what collaboration is, and can accept the personal and corporate benefits it can bring.

Before we look at what initiatives a plan might include, it is useful to examine some generic and overarching issues in more detail.

### *Readiness Review*

It is imperative to understand how people will react to the implementation of a change programme. Many companies try to gain this understanding via a survey; however, as we saw earlier, this approach is not only inherently unreliable, but can provide a completely false picture of how people actually feel and might react to the change plan.

The readiness review is best carried out through discussions with a cross-section of staff, to gain a view of the level of support they will personally provide towards the envisaged changes and identify any 'big issues'; and this input can be used to design appropriate engagement and communication strategies and plans.

### *Engagement and Enrolment*

Not wishing to labour the point (but it really is absolutely critical!), the most important aspect of the change plan is the enrolment and engagement of everyone associated with, and affected by, the introduction of collaborative working. In any change plan, people are not engaged by:

- being told what's good for them
- having their objections ignored or marginalised
- being lectured to.

What does engage them in a powerful way is:

- being given the time and space to become part of the programme
- having their views listened to and acted upon
- where appropriate, having their ideas incorporated into the implementation plan
- where this is not possible, providing them with an explanation as to why not
- being treated and talked to as adults!

I have seen many change programmes where the senior leadership team, who are in effect the change sponsors, spend months devising the programme, carefully developing the concepts and philosophy, calculating the benefits, and planning the implementation programme. During this time, the workforce will undoubtedly become aware that 'changes' are planned, but are neither involved nor informed, yet are expected to accept the purpose and validity of the programme in a one-hour roll-out session. The senior leadership team are then left wondering why they are often met with a wall of objections and resistance.

It is more effective and logical for the programme's sponsors to spend time gaining the workforce's acceptance of the programme, together with a realistic understanding of the obstacles that might be encountered in its implementation. This means inverting the 'involvement pyramid', and spending more time talking to those who will be affected by the changes, rather than the senior leadership team talking amongst themselves!

## Creation of Change Terrorists

As we discussed earlier, one of the most important aspects to consider in any change process is the danger of marginalising people who raise issues or objections.

What has to be recognised is that, when any change is proposed, it is normal, and even healthy, for people to raise what they see as potential issues and problems. This is a protective reaction to ensure that any perceived threats can be identified and dealt with.

The danger comes in trying to deal with these objections by either ignoring or negating them by referencing the overriding commercial advantages. Whilst this might silence the objectors in the short term, because they cannot disagree with the obvious organisational benefits, they nevertheless retain what they feel are legitimate objections, and therefore only become superficial supporters, when in fact they have simply gone 'underground' and become at best passive objectors and at worst 'change terrorists'.

Change terrorists are those who have been forced to become compliant by the weight of corporate argument, but who fundamentally disagree with the proposed changes, and will therefore seek to undermine the change programme at a later date to legitimise their own objections. Their tacit agreement merely gives them time to prepare an armoury of negative 'hand grenades' to be launched at an appropriate opportunity in the future, in order to derail the programme.

What is required is to accept the legitimacy of any objections, as they are real to the objector. Listen to them and encourage people to articulate their objections in an atmosphere of concern and empathy for their point of view. This can be a cathartic experience; once the objection is acknowledged and taken seriously, it can often gradually evaporate over time and eventually disappear. However, by ignoring it there is the danger of deepening their feelings of resentment, which will manifest itself in opposition to the programme and the people who sponsor it.

Taking objections seriously, even if not necessarily agreeing with them, and gradually referring to the potential advantages can help to put these objections into perspective. Hopefully they will eventually dissolve and be replaced by an acceptance of the benefits, and opponents will eventually become supporters of the programme.

### Fishes and Sharks

Another way of describing dissenters is to see them as 'sharks'. All change programmes endeavour to ensure everyone is aligned and swimming in the same direction, albeit at different speeds. There are occasions, however, when everyone appears to be swimming in the same direction, but where in reality some disguise their negativity, opposition and even resentment – these are the 'sharks' disguised as fish, and they are ready to attack at any time, but their disguise enables them to blend in with the main shoal. Only by having probing conversations with them – which, like X-rays, can expose their true feelings and intent – can the sharks be identified and action be taken to deal with their concerns.

## The Change Fallacy

When dealing with change, many papers and books cite the fact that people resist change, and indeed in most companies this becomes a corporate mantra, but it is wholly and totally false.

Give people a new piece of technology and they usually adapt to its use very quickly, because they see it as adding advantages to their way of life. For example, when presented with a new phone with new applications, they quickly grasp the opportunity to learn how to use it for their personal advantage. People taking up new positions in a company are energised by the change, and rise to the challenge.

People do not inherently resist change; they normally find it exciting and stimulating. What demotivates them, and can manifest itself in negativity, cynicism and oppositional behaviour, is being forced to adapt to changes where they have not been involved in their inception, development or application.

## Dealing with Resistors

There will be some individuals who remain strong objectors to the changes proposed and develop an oppositional mindset, which means they will twist every positive to a negative in the pursuit of standing firm and not having to agree to the changes proposed.

It is important to know when to listen to these objections so the objectors do not become change terrorists or sharks, but it's also important to know when it is necessary to accept their objections and move on. Indeed, continually giving additional information to counter their objections can sometimes simply provide them with more opportunity to cast negative aspersions on the programme.

Whilst carrying out the early engagement phases of a change programme with a beverage canning company, I was asked to spend a day with the quality assurance team, a group of young graduates who had clearly developed a negative group mindset and were negative and oppositional towards anything the company did or said. This mindset was so ingrained that it had distorted their view of everything the company did or said!

During the morning session I offered a number of positives from the company's perspective. For example, they had received a 5% salary increase when inflation was 2%, but this was countered with: "But the executives received 15%." I also mentioned that it was generous of the company to give every employee free shares, but this was countered by them saying that the leadership had been given millions of pounds of stock options. My final attempt was to 'suggest' that the free beer allowance of four cases per month was generous, and this provoked silence, which was only eventually punctuated by someone suggesting that the beer was about to go out of stock and that the company would have had to throw it away anyway, and incur additional cost, so the staff were doing them a favour by carrying it out the door!

My only counter to this was to use shock tactics, as I was beginning to feel that I was feeding their negativity. I put some cash behind the bar and after lunch told them they had a negative mindset which they needed to reflect on, and that if they didn't change they would waste their obvious talents and potential. I suggested that over a few drinks they took time out for some deep reflection, which would not be helped by me appearing to adopt a company stance.

It seemed to have the right effect, as they were stunned by my tactics, and I was gratefully informed by their manager of their positive change in attitude when they returned to work.

## Stakeholder Analysis

Stakeholder mapping is a conventional initiative in any transformation or change plan and is designed to gauge individual and group feelings and levels of support for the changes. The difference when planning a collaborative change programme is that different people and groups will have different views on:

- what collaboration is
- how it should be used
- what its potential is
- how it will affect processes, procedures, systems, behaviours and relationships.

When introducing a new IT system, it is relatively easy for everyone to develop a 'shared mental model' of the new system's functionality and its impact on organisational processes and procedures; however, as we have discussed earlier, collaboration is a new capability, and people have the freedom to hold their own personal views on how it can be applied.

It is therefore critical to provide all stakeholders with the opportunity to reflect on how the capability can be used, so that eventually there emerges a coalescence of views on the benefits and overall need for the programme. The stakeholder mapping process must therefore be much more thorough than it is in conventional change programmes, and it must be recognised that different people and groups will move at a different pace, and some will need to have more communication and discussion, and require more convincing, than others to become active supporters.

## Communications Strategy and Plan

The change plan will necessarily contain a robust communications strategy using an array of conventional communication vehicles, such as posters, newsletters, team briefs and 'town halls'.

However, the main distinguishing feature of a communication plan associated with a collaboration programme is the greater emphasis placed on initiatives that provide the opportunity for two-way discussions, designed so that people can understand the concepts and appreciate the benefits whilst at the same time airing their objections, concerns and fears. It is imperative to avoid 'sheep-dipping' people through a communication process – expecting them to understand and appreciate the concept and benefits via a one-hour, one-way presentation.

Another point that needs to be considered, and yet is often the so-called 'elephant in the room', is that the main communicator of the programme needs to be someone who is wholly and genuinely respected, and not someone who is seen purely as a corporate mouthpiece preaching corporate policy without expecting anyone to raise issues or concerns.

There is always a possibility that, if the main communication process involves a presentation to large groups, some individuals will remain silent and not want to raise objections for fear of being cast as 'oppositional irritants', a status which, they might feel, could adversely damage their reputation within the organisation and potentially affect their career progression.

## Presentational Style

The more powerful and polished the presentation, and the more graphs, diagrams and other sophisticated graphics it contains, along with quantifiable and apparently indisputable evidence for supporting the adoption of the proposal, the more it will silence the audience through 'presentational intimidation'.

Whilst those responsible for this presentational intimidation may have had laudable intentions, and perceive their work as being highly professional, polished, comprehensive and persuasive, so expecting it to engender enthusiasm and total agreement, it might well have a negative effect by making it impossible for people to raise emotional objections which they have difficulty quantifying or articulating against a background of overwhelming and apparently irrefutable facts.

It is akin to the technique of a company selling a time-share property by making a compelling and persuasive presentation on the advantages of participating in their scheme, stressing the opportunity to return to a favourite holiday destination and linking it with associated financial advantages, making the prospective buyer feel virtually incapable of declining the irresistible offer – and that, if they do, they are in some way intellectually inadequate in not understanding and accepting the compelling case! Speaking up is difficult. Having been pitched at several times in my lifetime by timeshare professionals, I deal with their pressurising sales tactics by agreeing with the concept, but adding that I have no spare funds – at all!

Comprehensive communication presentations are to some extent a patterned organisational behaviour. Most companies' communication vehicles, such as team briefs and town halls, are 95% provision of information and only 5% questions, on the assumption that the information provided will cover what people would like to know. This balance is often repeated when communicating a collaborative change plan, which is wholly inadequate. Instead what is required is 20% presentation of concept and plans and 80% discussion. What often sustains this imbalance towards information overload, particularly in large organisations, is that they have constructed a powerful internal communications team whose primary raison d'être is to help produce presentations which act to encourage 'talking to' and discourage 'talking with'.

Indeed, whilst this pattern is inappropriate for communicating plans to introduce collaborative working, it is also possibly inappropriate for traditional communications within organisations (such as town halls and team briefs). The senior leaders decide what they think their audience needs to know, rather than adopting a completely different approach by asking for questions either ahead of the event or just before it begins, then responding to these questions, and finally providing a short statement explaining what they think the audience needs to know.

## Prevailing Leadership Style

When introducing any transformation or change programme, the prevailing leadership style of the organisation has to be taken into account and the programme designed to accommodate it. The prevailing style might range from command and control, through participation and involvement, to complete consensus.

In command and control organisations, the tendency will be to design and implement the programme with minimal engagement, marginalising any emotional issues; this runs the risk of alienating individuals or groups, which will ultimately cause problems when using this new capability.

At the other end of the spectrum are consensus-style organisations. Whilst there might be a bias towards the communication process here, providing opportunities for wide-ranging discussions, any group could oppose the programme at any stage, which means that, although there may be initial agreement, objections can surface at any time and the programme can consequently be derailed.

Throughout the programme there needs to be a continual review of developing attitudes and emerging issues, and the programme flexed and adjusted to accommodate them.

## Use of Change Specialists

Given the many demands on all stakeholders in any modern organisation, the introduction of transformation and change initiatives often needs to be supplemented by using change specialists, who can provide appropriate support and guidance. That said, they should not become the managers of the implementation programme, as this role is best assumed by internal staff, who will remain after the changes have been installed. There is an inherent danger in letting the management of the programme be undertaken by transient personnel, as once they leave any gains could be subject to regression as they might not be sustained or supported by local management.

As we have already seen, it is also imperative to recognise the different types of change programmes mentioned earlier, these being:

- process
- technology
- organisational
- capability.

These need to be supported by change specialists with different skills and expertise as follows:

- process changes by individuals with business systems expertise
- technological changes by people who understand the technology being installed
- organisational changes by specialists with a blend of skills who can understand how the changes might affect new roles and responsibilities, as well as how the changes might be perceived by different stakeholders

- Change specialists supporting a capability change programme like collaboration need an understanding of each of these skills, together with a high level of empathy and an ability to provide the requisite coaching support to enable others to become proactive and self-motivated and able to see the benefits of installing the new capability, and also to possess the ability to understand different people's perspectives.

Beware of the consultancy organisation that offers the same person for all types of assignments! I have omitted the name in order to protect the innocent, but I encountered one individual on four different assignments: he turned up to support a maintenance strategy programme, a process redesign assignment, an IT implementation assignment and finally a collaborative environment programme. He survived each and was able to provide some input, but most importantly was light enough on his feet to skate on thin ice.

## Don't Rely on Gimmicks

Endeavour to make the change programme as natural as possible, and do not introduce or rely on any gimmicks.

In one change programme I was unable to recover from a gimmicky introduction, which involved displaying large posters across the factory which proclaimed "Beware: The Alligator Is Coming", with no explanation. This was intended to make people excited, interested and energised;

but then, after a month, it was announced that the alligator had arrived in the form of a well-intended group of external consultants, who embarked upon engagement workshops around the need for change. The workshops were ridiculed, as people felt that the process had treated them like children and demeaned their input as rational adults and experienced and skilled operation team leaders.

## It's Not What You Do, It's The Way That You Do It

Any change programme – and collaborative change is no exception – is moving the organisation towards a desired culture, so when planning and delivering the programme, it is important that it is carried out in a way which supports the attainment of the desired culture.

This means that, if the desired culture is one of sustained performance improvement through proactive, continuous improvement, and one element is the design of an external visit programme in order to gain experiences from other organisations, rather than the leadership team simply identifying visit targets and making a visit themselves, it might be designed in a way that encourages the inculcation of the desired culture by:

- asking team members:
  o what business processes need to be improved
  o which companies might be exemplars in these areas
- forming a visit team
- getting the team to arrange the visit

- the team reporting what they have learned back to the leadership team, and making appropriate recommendations.

If carried out in this way, this simple initiative encourages participation, involvement, research and communication – all critical elements of attaining the desired culture.

| KEY MESSAGES AND QUESTIONS |
| --- |
| • Collaboration is a capability |
| • The introduction of collaboration needs a bias towards education |
| • Ensure people understand and agree with the concepts of collaboration before moving on to implementing the programme |
| • Don't move too fast, as people will jump off the 'change train'! |
| • Involve people at every stage, and be genuine |
| • Beware of 'change terrorists' – identify them and convert them |
| • People do not resist change – they just resent not being involved |
| • Don't use presentational intimidation to gain acceptance |
| • Don't use change specialists to lead the programme |
| • Beware the consultancy organisation that never says no! |

# 6

## COLLABORATIVE ENVIRONMENTS

As mentioned earlier, it is worth taking some time to discuss the use of collaborative environments. These are technology-enabled areas that provide visual, data and audio connectivity between remote sites, variously described by companies as advanced collaborative environments (ACEs), integrated collaborative environments (ICEs), collaborative work environments (CWEs) etc.

In addition to these technology-enabled 'rooms', collaborative environments can be extended to include other people or groups who might only have periodic interaction within the enabled areas and are based outside the rooms.

These environments typically connect operational teams with their first-line support colleagues who can provide immediate technical support services. They also act as a conduit to connection with functional teams who might work on longer-term tasks.

The front-line support teams in effect become the focal point between the operational groups and the functional groups, as shown in the diagram on the next page.

The operational teams will have continuous discussions with their first-line support colleagues about emerging issues. The first-line support teams can then deal with these issues in one of four ways:

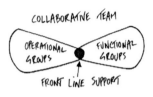

- tackle the issues themselves
- pass them on to a functional team
- pass them back to the operational teams
- form a team from all parties to deal with them at a later date.

Deciding who should tackle the problem requires knowledge of who has the right technical skills and time available, and also a high level of interpersonal skills to decide and gain agreement on who is the most suitable person or group to deal with the issue.

## One-Team Feel

Two or more remote groups that are joined together to form a collaborative environment need to develop a 'one-team feel', as they are not only in contact to discuss and solve problems that arise on a daily basis, but also have continual visual and audio connectivity. The feeling of being part of one team can be reinforced by individuals on both sides of the virtual environment with visual connectivity acting as if they are physically co-located, even in the simplest ways: for example, by acknowledging each other in the morning and saying goodbye in the evening! In other words, acting as if they actually are in the same room.

One important issue is that this collaborative group should not become, or even appear to become, elitist, and so ostracise functional teams which provide sporadic and as-required services. I have seen functional teams start to feel as though they are second-class citizens, and their sporadic interactions can make them feel outside the main group and therefore lack allegiance to the aims and objectives of the collaborative team, resulting in them not being galvanised to deliver quality work on time.

It is therefore important to make functional teams feel included by encouraging them to attend key meetings, and ensure that their contribution is recognised and they are included in celebratory and social events.

## Behavioural Protocols

Working and living in a collaborative environment is much like being in a large, open-plan office, the only difference being that the enlarged group is connected virtually. So, although you can see and interact with other remote team members at any time, albeit you can't physically touch them, you do need to treat them and behave as if they were in the same room.

Some organisations who set up collaborative environments feel the need to create and display some form of special behavioural charter dedicated to the expected norms of behaviour in the environment. This trend has become quite commonplace; however, it implies that the environment is something different and that any agreed ways of working within the rest of the organisation are somehow inappropriate.

To some extent, the need to create a specific behavioural charter infers that the act of collaboration is unusual, and even unnatural, and that the normal ways of interacting, talking to people and forming relationships will not naturally follow conventional standards, with people needing to be reminded how to act respectfully and courteously.

My own view is that the creation of a behavioural charter specifically for a collaborative environment infers that the environment really is different and is somewhere you cannot be yourself; instead, you have to live by special behavioural rules. This in itself can create anxiety and lay the foundations for personal confusion and potential friction.

That said, given that collaboration involves joining groups together that have different ways of acting and behaving, it might be useful to carry out a periodic review (as for any group) to ensure that there are no emerging relationship issues that, if left unattended, could impinge upon and adversely affect performance.

## Relationships

Gradually, relationships between groups connected within the environment can become very strong; however, this does not lessen the need to take time out to plan and hold team-building and socialisation events, which can shorten the relationship-building process and help lay the foundations for the creation of a truly high performance team – something we will discuss later.

## Interventions

As in an open-plan office environment, when making interventions in the collaborative environment you should simply use courtesy and common sense, and in particular remember to:

- check to see if people appear to be free before initiating an intervention
- clearly state what the purpose of the intervention is
- don't feel the need to stay connected, and so potentially 'steal' people's time
- if appropriate, send a very brief email as a reminder of any agreed actions
- if the intervention is a conversation between two people, be careful not to conduct it in a way which disturbs others in the environment who are not a party to the conversation – exactly as you would in a conventional office
- if a guest arrives in one side of the environment, make sure they are also introduced to the other side of the environment, as you would do if they were in the same room.

## Meetings Within the Collaborative Environment

Clearly, a number of formal meetings will take place within the environment, and it is important to ensure that, if the meeting only involves a few people from each side, it is conducted in a separate area so that it does not disturb other people in the environment. Also, because there will be a number of ad hoc interactions, it is worth reviewing the entire meeting structure and schedule, since it is quite possible that some existing formal meetings could either be shortened or abandoned altogether.

The one meeting that should be sacrosanct and attended by as many group members as possible is the daily meeting to review progress, allocate actions and celebrate success. This short (15–30 minutes) meeting is akin to a sporting team's group huddle before a game. It not only provides the opportunity to review business and performance, but also acts as a strong mechanism to bond people together and encourage a shared allegiance.

## Connectivity Quality

It is absolutely essential to ensure that the screen resolution and audio quality are of an exceptional standard. If second-rate equipment is sourced in order to reduce costs, and the image quality is compromised and the audio is not clean and crisp, this will reinforce the fact that the groups you are joining together are in fact separate and discrete and not united.

## Default Displays

Large screens are normally used within the collaborative environment to share data between remote groups during problem-solving tasks. However, when the screens are not being used in real time, their default displays should be the same on both sides of the environment to show current performance. In other words, they should show 'the score in the game', helping to unite both sides and reinforce that they are indeed one team trying to achieve a common goal.

## Personality Types

Behaving appropriately is a prerequisite for engendering constructive and harmonious working relationships in any team, and when working collaboratively it is unsurprising that there are certain personality types that appear to integrate and work more effectively within the environment. As collaboration necessitates continual interaction and intervention, to both give and receive support, the individuals who seem more comfortable with, and who can adjust more easily to, collaborative working, are those who have:

- natural joining skills
- high emotional intelligence
- resilience
- strong empathy
- the ability to deal with people from a variety of different organisational and cultural backgrounds.

On the other hand, individuals who struggle to settle into collaborative working are those who tend to have:

- a low tolerance of ambiguity
- strong and intractable views and opinions
- low personal empathy and sensitivity.

## Collaborative Roles

As in any team, individuals will play a number of roles, often described in the literature by referencing personality types using analysis tools such as Belbin or Myers Briggs. However, in collaborative working these descriptions are often inappropriate, as they do not take into account the effect of behaviour on the dynamic situation prevalent in collaboration. In collaboration, the effect of positive and negative behaviours will be accentuated, as individuals have the opportunity to influence and affect the opinions, attitudes and style of a wider group.

Given below are a few collaborative roles identified as potentially positive and negative.

| POSITIVE | | NEGATIVE | |
|---|---|---|---|
| Natural leaders | These team members provide focus, purpose and motivation | Time-stealers | Such individuals steal people's time, diverting attention from delivery, causing disturbance and disruption |
| Positive energisers | Some people have the ability to energise groups, and in collaboration they are particularly necessary to create a positive atmosphere | Social butterflies | These individuals have a need to continually discuss social, personal and non-business related topics, which distracts others from focusing on delivery, with the collaborative environment providing them with a captive audience |
| Constructive challengers | The input from these individuals can ensure that new ways of working and new processes can be devised and delivered by challenging the status quo | Gossips | Collaborative working provides gossips with more feedstock and opportunity and a larger captive audience to promulgate their stories |

| POSITIVE | | NEGATIVE | |
|---|---|---|---|
| Silent deliverers | There will be people in the team who might prefer to work in isolation, but who can cope and be exceptionally valuable members of any collaborative team if they are only disturbed when appropriate | Negative cynics | Some people are naturally inclined to be cynical about any new initiative or change, and collaborative working provides them with more opportunity to fuel their cynicism |
| Integrators | These are people who have a very strong network outside of the environment and can use this network to facilitate periodic and necessary inclusion of other specialists | Interlopers | The environment tends to attract individuals who are drawn by the activity and perceived kudos of the collaborative environment itself; these individuals must arrive with a positive contribution rather than as opportunistic interlopers |

## Dealing with Resistance

Any change programme will produce some degree of personal resistance. However, there is one area when introducing collaboration that requires special attention, as it provokes passionate negativity, often bordering on irrational hostility, and it is the use of cameras to create visual capability.

I have seen normally rational, competent, model employees turn passionately oppositional to the adoption and use of cameras to provide visual connectivity between remote groups, and have even witnessed their resistance manifesting itself in deactivating the camera, putting a temporary cover over the lens, pointing it to the ceiling or, in one extreme case, cutting the cables – effectively sabotage!

These feelings of negativity possibly emanate from the negative association of the use of cameras for surveillance purposes or for catching speeding motorists. Whilst this is clearly not the case in the use of cameras which enable visualisation between remote groups, unfortunately the associations are still there. This sense of being under surveillance is further reinforced when the image from the camera is displayed onto a screen; people then perceive them as like TV screens, which are normally passively watched. Furthermore, cameras traditionally take pictures that are stored and distributed to a wider audience at a later date.

All these associations often serve to make people refer to the visual capability in collaboration as being like 'Big Brother'; one person once referred to the office where the collaborative environment was being installed as "the George Orwell House"!

What many people seem incapable of comprehending, blinded by their heightened sensitivity and emotions, is that the cameras are, in effect, simply removing the physical wall between groups to create a virtual open-plan office. It is interesting that in a conventional open-plan office no one would think of staring at another person, but people fear this in a virtual office. Many people will agree to the need for visual capability, but request that the cameras remain off, and only be activated when they need to talk to someone. This is akin to having curtains around your desk in an open-plan office, which remain drawn unless you want to talk to someone!

When dealing with resistance in general it is also important to remember that people rarely give you the real reason for their objections, but rather proffer a view for not supporting the programme that they feel will be accepted as legitimate. This can result in the sponsors of the programme trying to deal with the voiced objection and, once dealt with, being surprised that resistance remains.

For example, when introducing collaboration it could be that people will cite as the reason for their objection the feeling that collaboration will result in them being disturbed, when their real objection is antipathy towards another individual or group; so any attempt to deal with the cited objection of being disturbed will not solve the underlying and unarticulated real reason.

## Taking the Credit

When working collaboratively it is easy to steal the ideas of others and claim credit for them yourself, as information freely passed between groups and individuals can be hijacked at any time by people who wish to portray themselves in a better light – so be careful that people do not poach the ideas of others and claim them as their own!

## Evaluation of the Environment

Collaborating provides groups with the opportunity for far more effective team working, and hence the attainment of improved efficiencies and commercial performance. However, the novelty of this working environment can cause some interpersonal friction, leading to misunderstandings, especially when the roles and responsibilities are unclear and people are getting used to interacting with other groups with different cultures.

It is therefore useful to carry out periodic reviews to bring any interpersonal, behavioural or relationship issues to the surface and design and implement appropriate interventions. This also provides a mechanism to identify and explore potential opportunities to extend the use of the collaborative capability.

The input for this review, like the culture review discussed earlier, should be collected via a combination of:

- one-to-one discussions
- attendance at meetings
- observations of the collaborative environment in daily use
- evaluation of meeting structures and business processes.

The review should provide a quantifiable output that can be categorised under a variety of headings, which will enable any emerging relationship or behavioural issues to be identified and addressed, ensuring that collaborative working supports the development of a cohesive and united team.

Given below are examples of some of the areas that need to be reviewed.

| COLLABORATIVE WORKING REVIEW | |
|---|---|
| Behaviours | How people are acting and relating with each other |
| Interventions | How and when interventions are made |
| Performance measures | What performance measures are used to drive improvements |
| Inclusion of third parties | To what extent third parties are encouraged to use the collaborative environment |
| Occupancy | To what extent the collaborative environment contains people with the right levels of skills and experience |
| Leadership support | How involved the senior leadership team is in promoting the use of the environment |
| Team working | What impact the environment has on team working |
| Interactions | How positive, harmonious and effective the interactions are between the remote teams |
| Use of data feeds | What use is made of data feeds to input into action plans to improve performance |

| KEY MESSAGES AND QUESTIONS |
|---|
| • Ensure that people who only occasionally use the environment are welcomed |
| • Don't create a behavioural charter – it makes collaborative working look unnatural |
| • Make interventions as you would do in a normal open-plan office environment |
| • Treat people as if they actually were in the same room – say hello and goodbye! |
| • Use default displays to show performance progress |
| • Cameras are only there to bring down a 'wall' – they do not take still pictures or encourage people to stare! |
| • Don't deactivate the visual connectivity – it's like drawing curtains around your desk in an open-plan office |
| • Never use collaborative working to take credit for the work or ideas of others |
| • It is useful to carry out a periodic collaborative working review |
| • Ensure the audio and visual connectivity is high quality |
| • Beware of time-stealers and social butterflies |

# 7

# ORGANISATIONAL ISSUES

The introduction of collaborative working will high-light a number of organisational issues that need to be dealt with, and which will provide opportunities to further embed the new agreed ways of working and improve operational and commercial performance. These issues will vary, and will be dependent both on the degree of collaboration and the maturity and complexity of the organisation.

Given below are a few organisational issues that I have encountered in designing and installing collaborative working.

## Performance Appraisal Systems

All companies have some form of process for appraising individual performance against agreed delivery criteria. Through wider collaboration, people will impinge upon and hence affect the work of other functions and groups that would previously have been somewhat remote. Therefore, it follows that these previously more separate groups, whose performance is now influenced by and even dependent upon others, should be given the opportunity to provide input into the appraisal process.

My own view is that, in general, appraisal of performance should be an ongoing activity, and not confined to an annual or biannual basis. This is even more important in collaborative working, when it is imperative to evaluate not only each individual's contribution, but also the effect they are having on team dynamics and, if necessary, to provide appropriate coaching support to ensure they understand the effect their impact is having so they can make the appropriate behavioural modifications.

## Meeting Structures

Once collaboration has been embedded, it is useful to review the organisation's meeting structures, to decide whether they might be modified in terms of attendance, frequency, inputs, outputs and deliverables.

Since some interactions, decisions and subsequent actions will be facilitated by collaboration, it could well mean that meetings can be truncated to free up time to deal with emerging issues. In addition, it is useful to evaluate who should attend meetings and what decisions need to be made. All too often, the tendency is to expand the number of attendees at a meeting purely because the collaborative capability makes it possible. It is also likely that some meetings might become redundant as the issues they once addressed at formal meetings are now dealt with in real time.

It is also important at all meetings to appoint one overall leader, as the remote groups have a tendency to each appoint their own leader, which can cause confusion about who is actually responsible for the chairmanship of each meeting to ensure it delivers the desired output.

## Reporting Structures

Traditionally, and naturally, most organisations are structured on a regional or functional basis, with solid reporting lines to facilitate the application of management control and reporting systems, and dotted lines to indicate the resources available from support functions. However, the widespread installation of collaborative working in a geographically dispersed organisation provides the opportunity to cluster and manage remote groups based on their technological similarities. A global oil and gas major, for example, might decide to manage deep-water floating production and storage facilities in one group, and gas production facilities in another.

## Decision Rights

In steady-state operations it is clear who makes what decisions, and such matters are clearly defined according to an organisational blueprint. However, once you introduce collaborative working, more people are inputting into issues, and it can become rather confusing as to who is responsible for making the ultimate decision. This confusion can often result in the decision-making process migrating to those with the stronger personalities.

When introducing collaborative working, the best course of action is to retain the existing decision rights whilst receiving additional input from other functions, and then, if appropriate, gradually refining the decision-making process and adjusting the new decision rights as appropriate.

## Reward Systems

When joining two groups together you are by definition intentionally making them feel like one united team.

This will lead individuals in the remote teams to become closer colleagues and to share information regarding their terms and conditions of employment. In the event that you are joining two teams together which you ideally want to be seen as equal, but where there is disparity in the reward systems, this can lead to the lower-paid team feeling undervalued in comparison to the other group. This can be particularly acute when joining two countries together, where on occasion there can be a vast disparity in pay, a feature not borne out of company policy, but observance of local pay norms.

| KEY MESSAGES AND QUESTIONS |
| --- |
| • Ensure the performance appraisal system includes input from all stakeholders |
| • Review meeting structures |
| • Keep the decision rights as is, and gradually refine on an as-required and agreed basis |
| • Look at the remuneration differences of groups being joined together and ensure they are not causing resentment |

# 8

## CREATING HIGH
## PERFORMANCE TEAMS

The primary and ultimate purpose of collaboration is to help the wider team achieve its stated goals and objectives, and to engender a culture of continuous improvement so that it becomes and remains a high performance team.

The term 'high performance team' is in popular usage and is regularly bandied around, and has become standard company parlance, as if in the hope that, if it is mentioned enough, the group will somehow morph into achieving exceptional performance. However, to actually achieve it is difficult, as the team will first have to admit that it is not already a high performance team and then identify and articulate its shortcomings – a task which many teams will find too painful, if not impossible, to do.

Hopefully, this book has stimulated you to understand the part that collaboration can play in creating truly high performance teams, and also some of the concepts behind collaboration, and will encourage organisations to pursue what is really just a natural progression in the communication process. As has been mentioned before, many of the advantages of implementing collaborative working come from the emotional benefits gained in creating a sense of belonging, a desire to attain a common goal, and an enthusiasm to share in its success – all essential elements of creating a high performance team.

In my experience, if introduced correctly and then nurtured, collaboration can be one of the most powerful enablers in the creation of united teams, so it is probably now useful to look at the fundamental elements of a high performance team. In essence, they can be distilled into and discussed under nine main headings:

- everybody knows the challenge
- there is an accepted and respected leader
- there is appropriate individual behaviour
- people accept personal accountability
- performance is monitored, measured and displayed
- communication is authentic, plain and simple
- a team's performance is compared against another's
- contributions are recognised and rewarded
- success is celebrated.

Clearly, these will be supported by the conventional business processes around effective people selection, appropriate ongoing training, appraisals, reward and recognition schemes and succession planning, but let's look at each of the other issues identified above.

## Knowing the Challenge

High performance teams know what they are trying to achieve. Whilst this might seem rather obvious and a little trite, you will be surprised at the number of teams whose members find it difficult, if not impossible, to effectively and succinctly articulate precise and unambiguous, quantifiable targets and current performance.

When carrying out early engagement or conducting readiness reviews for collaboration, in confidential one-to-one discussions I have on many occasions asked the questions: "What is the team trying to achieve?" or "How are you performing this year so far against your defined targets?", and the reactions can be like a rabbit caught in the headlights! People are often unable to provide any meaningful answers, but merely react with phrases like "I think we're doing well" or "I don't think we've had a very good time recently". The process is rather akin to asking a football player "Where are you in the league?" and getting the answer "Somewhere near the top, I think!"

To extend this sporting analogy, I have often found that people who have scant knowledge of the performance of their work teams are nevertheless able to define the challenge and evaluate the progress of a sporting team they support. This would seem to indicate that they have strong concern about, interest in and allegiance to a sporting team, which simply provides them with entertainment, but don't appear to have the same level of attachment to the company that provides them with the finances to follow the team they support!

The primary challenge the team faces will underpin the attitudes of individual team members and bond the team together. If they have a definable challenge, this will help to act as an inspirational motivator and provide meaning to their work. Without a challenge their efforts will become laborious, with no consequence or purpose; it is therefore hardly surprising that this will lead to 'de-energisation', with individuals simply going through the motions. Knowing what they are trying to achieve will give them real purpose, enabling them to become truly engaged and sustain energy.

## Stretching Targets – Yes or No

It is common practice for most companies to set individuals and teams what have become known as 'stretch targets', in the hope that these will motivate them to be more diligent, conscientious and hard-working. The danger is that, if the targets are unrealistic or too demanding, people will become disillusioned and demotivated, leading to a sense of underachievement and inadequacy, resulting in a loss of energy, morale and motivation.

On the other hand, if the targets are realistic, the extra energy gained from success will make people work more diligently to achieve even higher performance. It seems to me that companies that set overly ambitious stretch targets do this in the mistaken belief that individuals are not intrinsically motivated, and will only work hard by being constantly pushed to achieve something that is potentially beyond their reach. This is untrue, as everybody gains satisfaction and enjoyment from work if it leads to achievement of a goal, and they will not simply stop work once the goal has been achieved, but will be galvanised to continue on past the original goal, motivated by a sense of success. It is based on the false premise that people are motivated by failure, and is akin to a child of 5 or 6 who is coping with an early reader book having it taken away and being set stretch targets to see if he or she can cope with, say, *Hard Times* or *Twelfth Night*.

## The Confusion Around Key Performance Indicators (KPIs)

Most teams are now familiar with the concept of establishing KPIs, with the underlying principle being 'the more the merrier'. These indicators are often displayed by using a traffic light system, with a desire for a sea of green. There is common confusion about the use and benefits of KPIs, and a misunderstanding of the difference between KPIs and team targets.

The introduction of KPIs and their monitoring and examination should be used to understand where resources need to be directed in order to improve individual skills, and where further training is needed to improve team performance. Using the traffic light system, it follows that you will want to have some KPIs that are amber and red in order to know where to direct scarce resources to improve performance. It further follows that, if all the KPIs are green, you are likely to simply sit back on your laurels, meaning that further improvements in performance will never occur!

I asked one control room operator who had over 20 KPIs displayed behind his panel what the figures meant. His reply was, "I haven't got a clue – I'm not even sure if the graph should be going up or down!"

To use another sporting analogy, a rugby team's primary target might be to win the league in order to gain promotion, but the KPIs would be around tackles made, tackles missed, line-outs won and lost, passes made and received, distance run etc. These would then be used to establish where the individuals need extra skills or fitness training to improve their current performance.

Individuals in a team are not motivated by KPIs, although as we have seen they do have a purpose. A team is motivated by a few (up to three) simple team targets, such as production rates, operational efficiency and safety performance, all of which can be monitored, measured and displayed.

## Leadership

Like any group, a collaborative team's performance will be significantly influenced by the leader's style. The leader will perform all the normal functions of setting strategy, goals and deliverables, as well as providing the necessary motivation and morale to ensure the team remains energised; but in collaborative working there is also a heavy coaching dimension to ensure that people interact in a positive, dynamic manner and form harmonious, effective working relationships with a wide variety of other teams and functions.

Every bookshop groans with tomes on leadership, but in my experience a truly high performance team needs a leader who:

- is authentic
- cares more about the performance of the team than his or her own career

- holds people truly accountable
- delivers on promises
- sets performance standards and measures progress
- trusts team members
- has personal integrity
- is respected
- (and most importantly of all) is inspirational.

Inspiration should not be confused with strength of personality. I have seen quiet, calm, reflective leaders provide strong inspiration, whereas gregarious, 'full-on' individuals can often create an overbearing sense of oppressive control. Inspirational leaders, by their personal demeanour, integrity and charisma, can create an atmosphere and culture that encourages team members to go the extra mile, not for their own benefit, or indeed for the leader's, but for the team itself.

Teams that have truly inspirational leaders will work as hard, if not harder, and with more dedication when the leader is not present, spurred on by a desire to personally not let the leader down, and wanting to have their efforts acknowledged on the leader's return. These inspirational leaders seem to stir the souls of individuals in a way which is difficult to explain or rationalise. It is not an acquired skill, but comes from the leader's capacity to engender an atmosphere where individuals feel they are genuinely respected and their efforts valued.

Another way of looking at inspiration is that it motivates individuals. There is no shortage of definitions of motivation in the literature, but the one I prefer is: "Motivation is the anticipation of future pleasure." So, an inspirational leader motivates people to want to come into work, as they anticipate it will be a pleasant experience; people will be motivated to go the extra mile if they know their efforts will be recognised and appreciated.

Inspirational leaders also have as their primary target the improvement of the team's performance, and nothing else. They do not look for opportunities for personal aggrandisement or to enhance their personal career prospects. Their sole focus is on the team's performance target, whereas some leaders will publicly claim this as their primary target, but will have a secondary agenda, possibly built around their own career progression, which means they might take their eye away from the main target and miss the bullseye!

There has been much discussion in the literature about the difference between an administrator, a leader and a manager. In my view it can be summarised as:

- administrators – apply processes and procedures
- managers – control
- leaders – inspire.

Using another sporting analogy (sporting analogies are often useful, since sports teams are always concerned with success, winning and celebration), it has always occurred to me as interesting that, if a football team underperforms, even for a short time, the board will quickly sack the manager. However, if a business team underperforms for a similar period, the company will seek to replace the workforce, leaving the manager in position to oversee the recovery – strange!

## Appropriate Individual Behaviour

It almost goes without saying that people need to behave in a way that is acceptable and respected so that they can integrate into and become valued members of the team, not only as individual contributors but also as facilitators of a spirit of mutual cooperation.

Interestingly, perhaps the most important aspect of individual behaviour is that no one ever sees or reflects on the effect their own behaviour has on team dynamics – because they are always there! An individual might attend a meeting which becomes derailed, confusing and ineffective, and then attend another meeting with the same result, but never reflect on why, or identify himself or herself as the primary cause, but simply come to the conclusion that the meetings are inherently poor!

The converse is also true: some people will provide energy, direction and focus in every meeting they attend, but sometimes do not recognise that they are the prime reason for this positive atmosphere. When these people leave the meeting and it gradually loses positive momentum and becomes more mundane and ponderous, they never see the effect, and cannot understand why the team isn't achieving more in their absence.

I was recently carrying out a culture/teamwork review and was in an operational control room talking to a group of technicians to gain an understanding of how they felt about working in the organisation. The conversation was very animated, interesting, open and informative, with people trusting the anonymity of the conversation; whilst they were not being disrespectful to the organisation, they were outlining some of their frustrations. In the middle of this energetic exchange the team leader appeared and everyone immediately went quiet, which prompted the Team Leader to say: "Come on lads, don't go quiet just because Paul's here", clearly blissfully unaware of the effect he had on his own team members!

## Energy-Hoovers

There are some people who can enter a room and unintentionally suck the energy from it and each individual in it until the group, once a balloon, becomes deflated. These are energy-hoovers.

Interestingly, these energy-hoovers may recognise the negative effect they are having on individuals and the team itself, and consequently often try to compensate by articulating and demonstrating their competence in their own role.

On one occasion I was providing coaching support for an operations team, and every Monday morning an energy-hoover always arrived late, full of negativity and criticism, and with an air of total despondency. The early positive banter in the group regarding the weekend's activities quickly evaporated as the energy was slowly removed by the energy-hoover's caustic, negative, hostile and almost venomous comments, so that one by one each individual became deflated.

Probably one of the most influential behavioural traits of any team member is the ability to remain optimistic in a range of situations. This is not to become the team clown or deluded, but merely to retain a positive attitude and approach.

## The Rule of 75

In dealing with behaviour it is dangerous to rely on people's own opinion of themselves about how good behaviour is, as they will tend to overestimate it, particularly in relation to others.

Indeed, this relates not only to behaviour and personal characteristics but to their performance of any activity or skill!

Out of interest I have asked countless groups, both work and social, to rate a non-work skill, such as their driving ability on a scale between 0 and 100, with 0 being the worst driver in the country and 100 the best. When people are asked where they see themselves on that spectrum, the average answer in any group is always around 75! You can extend this to how sensitive they are, how cooperative, how supportive etc., but the answer is always 75. I've carried out this exercise with numerous groups and rarely have I been able to find more than a handful of people who rate themselves below 50. However, by definition, if the average is 50, half the people in the world must be below 50 – but I can't find them!

## Two Choices!

Another facet of individual behaviour is that any trait can be described in either a positive or a negative way depending upon your feelings towards the person you are describing. A person can be described as thrifty or mean, observant or voyeuristic, a good communicator or verbose, supportive of management or sycophantic. It is therefore useful to check your own vocabulary when describing an individual to see whether your words are generally positive or negative, and review whether there is any correlation between your choice of language and your feelings towards that person.

## Accepting Personal Accountability

It might seem something of a tautology to talk about personal accountability when dealing with collaboration; however, the importance of accepting responsibility for personal delivery is even more critical in collaborative working as there is interdependency between people, and non-delivery by one party could quickly sever the chain, seriously adversely affecting the performance of the whole team.

This interdependency can again be usefully illustrated by reference to a sporting analogy. In golf teams people play as individuals and their results are aggregated. Moving up the interdependency ladder, a relay team is dependent upon each runner passing the baton to the next (something the British team were better at in the 4 x 100m men's Olympics final in Athens, when they beat the USA into second place, even though the Americans had the fastest individual runners). Even greater interdependence is demonstrated in a team game such as football, where the forwards are dependent upon getting the ball delivered to them by the backs so they can score. Finally, at the top of the ladder are activities which are totally interdependent, such as trapeze acts or pairs ice-skating, or the Red Arrows air display team.

It should therefore be accepted that, in addition to individuals accepting personal responsibility, there has to be personal accountability. There must be personal consequences for both under and over-delivery. If there is under-delivery there has to be an acceptance that there will be a discussion around the causes so that they can be eradicated, and where there is over-delivery there should be some form of recognition to act as positive reinforcement.

## Monitoring and Displaying Performance

Every high performance team should measure and display its performance against targets, but, rather similar to the case in understanding the challenge, many organisations I have been involved with over the years do not clearly display their performance against targets, either on a daily or cumulative basis. Or, to put it another way, no one seems to know the score in the game! They simply come to work, perform their tasks and leave, which is hardly a recipe for creating highly motivated individuals.

In discussing this with some teams I have often been told by the team leader that there is no need to display performance, as team members can easily find it on the corporate intranet. This is akin to a cricket spectator asking "What's the score?" and, rather than having it displayed on a scoreboard, being told to search for it on the team's website.

It is also powerful if the performance of a production operation is measured on an hourly basis, and then written up by hand with a felt-tip pen on a large paper display. Whilst this might fly in the face of high-tech computer-generated displays, the act of an individual personally writing up performance makes it come alive, and provides it with real meaning and immediacy. Not only does the output become personal, but people feel drawn to numbers that are both real and alive, as they have been inscribed by real people in real time and therefore cannot be ignored. If they exceed targets they will act as powerful motivators, and if they fall short they will serve to galvanise people to get back on track.

If you enter a team environment and cannot easily see its performance prominently displayed then the chances are that the team will probably be coasting: doing work, but not being highly galvanised or energised.

## Communication

Effective, authentic and natural communication is the lifeblood of any high performance team. The main dangers in corporate communications are:

- there is too much communication
- the mouthpieces are neither respected nor trusted
- there is a high reliance on corporate mantras, which are not reinforced by the leadership's behaviour
- there is too positive a spin, so 'elephants' remain in the room.

On a regular basis it is worth reviewing the communication messages, vehicles and their effects to ensure that any of these potential dangers are identified and actions taken to eradicate them.

## Meetings

We have already discussed the need to review meeting structures, composition and objectives in collaborative working, but it is worth discussing a few other issues concerning high performance teams.

What has to be accepted is that meetings are not necessarily value-adding work. Whilst problem-solving groups do add value, numerous meetings which discuss, plan and review performance do not. Interestingly, if a sporting team isn't performing well it takes action to improve skill levels, fitness and tactics, all of which will be activity based rather than conducted through meetings. Yet the opposite is true in many organisations, where performance improvement is often tackled by getting more information and holding more meetings to discuss the perceived problem, which results in less activity. This results in a downward spiral, where eventually meetings take the place of actions.

The antidote to this is to limit the number of hours per week each person spends in meetings. Once a figure is fixed at, say, 10 hours, and this is fully subscribed to, any new meetings which need to be accommodated must replace existing meetings.

## Comparing Team Performance

Any team has to have an opponent or 'enemy' that can be used to motivate team members and act as a focus for instilling a sense of allegiance, pride and belonging, as well as providing a sense of achievement in 'winning'.

In collaborative working, an organisation often brings together groups that might once have seen each other if not as enemies then at least as potential targets to apportion blame, as an excuse for their own poor performance.

Once the teams are joined together, the enemy has to be outside of the enlarged group, and this can act as a powerful motivator for comparing the team's performance against another group, either within the organisation or, more powerfully, outside it.

Even if the group has no equivalent competitors, either internally or in the wider marketplace, the 'opposition' could simply be poor performance.

## Acknowledging Contributions

When groups work in isolation it is relatively easy to identify who has contributed to what, and then acknowledge the contribution where appropriate. However, in effective collaboration numerous people will have made contributions, so it becomes somewhat difficult to readily identify those who actually made the most valuable input when a successful outcome has been achieved; indeed, on occasion it may be inappropriate to single one person out so the recognition and acknowledgement should be directed towards the team itself.

## Celebration of Success

It is essential that the team celebrates the achievement of milestones jointly, either by simple recognition by senior leaders or at offsite socials.

The purpose of celebrating success is to publicly recognise the achievement. If no celebration is organised, and the milestone passes without mention, it can serve to instil feelings that the efforts are not appreciated. This will tend to demotivate both individuals and groups, leading to a subconscious lack of diligence, attentiveness and effort, which will undoubtedly lead to poorer performance in the future.

Conversely, public celebration provides powerful positive reinforcement, so that people feel genuinely appreciated; it will sustain and even increase their efforts through the hope and expectation that further work will lead to similar experiences.

One critical issue that is often overlooked is that it is not merely important but imperative that the leader fronting the events that acknowledge contributions and celebrate success is respected by the recipients.

I have seen many celebratory events at which the person or group being thanked would rather not have received them from someone with whom they felt no personal bond or had no respect for; indeed, on occasions where groups collectively hold negative feelings towards the company or a specific leader, by accepting the accolade they believe they risk showing what they perceive to be an unhealthy allegiance to a body or person that they feel antipathy towards.

It is also important to conduct celebratory events publicly in a manner in which everyone feels included. For example, it is not always appropriate to celebrate in a pub or restaurant setting, where the consumption of too much alcohol can make some people in the group feel uncomfortable.

Finally, let's look at what happens when people are looking forward to a celebration associated with milestone achievements but the milestone is then missed, leading to the joint disadvantages of disappointed individuals coupled with the consequences of poor performance.

It is essential not to move the goalposts, pretend that the milestones didn't exist or, worse, lower the bar or increase the time needed to achieve the stated goals. What is required is to openly discuss the position at a normal team meeting and seek the reasons why the targets were not met, so that people's views can be heard, and so they can decide what actions need to be taken to meet future milestones, and where appropriate, also thank people for the efforts they have made.

## The Danger of Double Standards

Mention was made earlier of problems that arise if there are double standards in an organisation, and in particular when one group feels that another group is receiving unmerited privileges, which leads to feelings of resentment. Apart from remuneration, which should be based on value to the organisation, any other 'perk' must be seen as necessary for the individual or group to carry out their role for the benefit of the organisation.

Whilst carrying out a team review for a major brewing company, in an early conversation with a shop steward we touched on the topic of training, which elicited a response from him which was then echoed by others, and had become a mantra for the illustration of double standards: "Anyone from the shop floor has to jump through hoops to go on any course, and when you give valid reasons why you need to go they say there's no money, but management could go on a course on fly-fishing and ferret-hunting!"

| KEY MESSAGES AND QUESTIONS |
| --- |
| • Do all team members know the individual and team targets? |
| • Don't expect all KPIs to be green! |
| • If you are a leader, are you inspirational? |
| • Are team members truly held accountable for their delivery? |
| • Are there any 'energy-hoovers' in your team? |
| • Do you overestimate your behavioural strengths? |
| • Does your team monitor and display performance? |
| • Do you have more than 10 hours of meetings each week? |
| • Who is your team's 'enemy'? |
| • Good leaders deliver on their promises |
| • When did you last celebrate success? |
| • Are there any double standards in your organisation? |
| • You never see the effects of your own behaviour |

# 9

## TEAM DEVELOPMENT

### Team Reviews

It is useful to take time out on a regular basis to review team dynamics. The input to this type of review can be obtained by observing group interactions, and the output then fed back both to individuals, in the form of facilitated coaching support, and to the group as a whole, by sensitively explaining how differences in style, attitudes and behaviours are impacting on team dynamics.

The output should also identify and encourage positive behaviours that are contributing to harmonious and supportive working relationships, and those behaviours that are impacting negatively on the team should also be identified and actions taken to modify them.

### Team-Building

Companies often feel that, to help establish strong personal bonds, team-building activities are an integral part of building a high performance team.

It is worth making a few points about classic team-building events, which often revolve around activities such as clay-pigeon shooting, paintballing, go-karting or ten-pin bowling. These are not actually team-building events at all, but social occasions which provide opportunities for a degree of personal bonding; however, they will not help people to realise how their own behaviour, attitudes and opinions affect others.

If an individual upsets people at work by exhibiting an attitude that exudes overconfidence bordering on arrogance, he or she is liable to act in exactly the same way when taking part in any social or leisure activity; in fact, these traits might even be exaggerated without the restriction of a working environment. Therefore, if people are aggressive at work, they are liable to be just as aggressive when ten-pin bowling, so such classic team-building events can actually worsen personal relationships.

In my experience there are three main types of group events:

- those that discuss and resolve issues
- ones that uncover, understand and solve interpersonal conflict
- those that provide people with the opportunity to build stronger personal bonds.

If you try to cover all these issues in one event, the result will at best lead to confusion and at worst serve to accentuate and deepen any personal friction or animosity.

What should be avoided at all costs is an event which is badged as simply a team-building event, and where there is no stated purpose. In that case, everybody comes with different issues to resolve and feels disappointed if they are not addressed. Another failing of most team-building events is a crowded agenda, which raises a plethora of new concerns and issues which cannot be addressed in the time available, and this can lead to disappointment and even resentment.

Before an issues-resolution event takes place, it is imperative that the issues are first identified so that people can reflect on how they might be resolved. You must also ensure that only these issues will be dealt with on the day.

In my experience team-building events fail because:

- one or two vocal people are allowed to dominate discussions
- there is a failure to recognise when there is a need for a break to re-energise or lighten the atmosphere
- there is a failure to recognise when it is beneficial for the event to be facilitated by a neutral person, so that it does not become dominated or overly influenced by the appointed leader.

If you find yourself at any team-building event where copious flip chart notes are made on what needs to change, the actions that need to be taken etc. and the team assistant is then asked to type them up and circulate them at the close of the session, the likelihood is that nothing at all will change. When the number of flip chart pages pinned around the room reaches 20, with probably 100 or so associated actions, just make your excuses and leave as nothing will happen! What is more effective is to agree three or four actions, assign champions and monitor progress at the next event.

## Being Together

The members of truly high performance teams enjoy being in each other's company – not necessarily agreeing, but finding interaction with other team members interesting, stimulating and energising. They actively look for opportunities to be in each other's company, naturally provide and receive advice, and choose to socialise together.

They also look for opportunities to promote the contribution of their team members to other individuals and groups, and will defend and protect members of the team if their work is challenged by others.

## Developing an External Perspective

High performance teams have the desire to search outside of their own organisation for new ideas, concepts, philosophies and activities to continually improve and enhance their own performance. This external perspective can be achieved in two main ways:

- Continually refreshing the team by recruiting and embedding people from other industries. Clearly this refreshment requires high staff churn, which may or may not be possible or even desirable, and also relies on the embedded team being able to listen to and accept the opinions and views that new members of staff bring from their external experiences.

- Developing an external visit and speaker programme, where groups identify team development needs and look for other industries which excel in these categories; arranging appropriate visits; agreeing what could be applied to effect improvements back at base; and devising appropriate implementation programmes. This can be paralleled by inviting external speakers from other sectors to share their experiences.

The main danger in an externalisation programme is that there is a tendency to arrange visits to, and get speakers from, companies which are perceived to be similar to your own organisation, when what is required is the complete opposite. Visiting a company which appears on the surface to have no association with your own will probably generate the deepest, most reflective, interesting and effective ideas. This is because if you visit companies similar to your own, your learning will be incremental, as you will merely add to your current knowledge base and not be encouraged to make the step-jumps in learning that come from visiting and talking to companies in different sectors.

An example is when I organised an external visit programme for a drinks company and we had a presentation from the manager of a major theme park, who stated that the company's main aim was to package and deliver fun. As part of his presentation he mentioned that every manager in the company had to spend at least four shifts per year on the front line, loading the public onto rides, to give them a taste both of the experience of what the company was actually delivering and the reactions from their fee-paying customers. This led the drinks company to embark upon a 'work experience for managers' programme, where every manager spent three 12-hour night shifts working as a production line assistant. The experience gave the managers insight into working a continental shift pattern and the effect it had on personal life. It also gave them an opportunity to bond with the workforce, and for the workforce to provide them with some real-time feedback on the company's style and performance.

## Traits of a High Performance Team

We have discussed the fundamental elements of a high performance team, from knowing the challenges to celebrating success. From my own experience, as well as attending to the issues we have already discussed, the major traits of a high performance team are that they:

- are energised by association with each other
- feel able to speak freely without fear of ridicule
- celebrate new members of the team joining with a social event, rather than confine it to leavers (which has always seemed rather strange to me)
- take a keen interest in the team's performance and progress once they have left
- develop empathy that allows them to know when to speak, when to listen, when to support and when to offer advice
- respect the leader personally rather than his or her positional authority
- are comfortable talking to more senior leaders without feeling the need to 'seek permission'
- deal with every issue even if on the surface some may appear 'too hot to handle'

- identify what they see as unnecessary corporate bureaucracy, processes or procedures, indicating where there are shortfalls and suggesting modifications, but never allowing them to dent personal morale
- proactively initiate reviews on how their personal style impacts on others
- respect other team members' time off, but nevertheless feel they can contact them in an emergency as the other party will accept that it is absolutely necessary.

Finally, the acid test is that they should seize every opportunity to socialise together – to test this, call an impromptu dinner at three days' notice and see how many people attend!

## The Rule of 10

To check whether you are in a high performance team you might ask yourself the following questions, giving yourself a score of between 1 and 10, with 1 being bad and 10 being good.

- How much do you enjoy coming into work?
- How much do you enjoy the company of other team members?
- How energised do you feel at work?
- How much respect do you have for your leader?
- If you go the extra mile, will it be recognised?

If your combined score is less than 10, you are probably demotivated and de-energised and are making yourself unwell, and it will probably be best if you look for a new opportunity, either in another function or another company!

| KEY MESSAGES AND QUESTIONS |
|---|
| • Carry out periodic team reviews |
| • Don't expect traditional team-building events to improve relationships |
| • Does your team actively seek opportunities to socialise? |
| • How does your team gain an external perspective? |
| • Can you identify and deal with any issue, or are some too hot to handle? |
| • If you don't enjoy coming to work or aren't energised by it you might be better off seeking a new team! |
| • Don't try to combine issue-resolution meetings with socialisation events |
| • Do you really enjoy coming into work? |

# 10

## STRIVING FOR EXCELLENCE

A truly high performance team strives for excellence. In fact, every organisation strives for excellence, although few achieve it. This is not the result of a lack of either desire or resources, but primarily because organisations fail to realise that the attainment of excellence is, in essence, a mindset change, and, whilst all the traditional business processes must be effective and efficient, they need to be paralleled with the attainment of excellence in all other aspects of the organisation's working life.

It is impossible for individuals to select where or when to be excellent. High performance teams can only achieve their full potential by operating within an organisation where excellence is the norm. For example, in a manufacturing organisation achieving world-class levels of production, performance will not be attained by dealing with the traditional business processes of operations, maintenance and planning alone; attention also needs to be given to achieving excellence in a whole range of other non-core business categories.

## The Excellence Maypole

Core business processes such as safety, reliability, operations and maintenance can be compared to the central pole of a maypole, with the attached ribbons being the enablers. Examples of these enablers would be:

- housekeeping
- meeting etiquette
- individual behaviour
- employee induction packs
- office environment
- catering arrangements
- work attire

as illustrated below.

EXCELLENCE MAYPOLE

An organisation's attempt to improve its core business processes and performance will eventually lead to the enabler ribbons becoming taut, so preventing any further improvement in performance. What is then required is to improve the performance of the enablers, so allowing continuous improvement of the core business processes.

## Attaining Excellence

To implement a programme of excellence, all the core business processes and enablers must be identified and excellence standards defined for each category. A review should then be carried out to establish the current state of each category, and actions planned that can move the organisation towards the desired excellence standard.

There is a danger that, in defining the excellence standards, an organisation will quite naturally work from within its own paradigm and be unable to easily move outside it so as to define what the ultimate excellence standard might be. For example, in one excellence programme I was involved with, a syndicate group working on the communication category defined excellence as the use of rigorous and multifaceted communication vehicles providing accurate information on all the company's activities, processes and procedures. However, if there is respect and trust between individuals and groups within the company, excellence in communication might be a move towards less communication, with individuals gaining much of what they need to know from trusted and respected ad hoc communications. So, the excellence standard might be less communication and not more.

Also required is a zero-tolerance approach in each category, so that it engenders the desired excellence mindset and ensures people recognise that they can't choose when and where to be excellent; instead, it becomes a standard personal norm. In companies which have attained excellence, people who subsequently join adhere to the excellence standards; in contrast, in companies which fall short of excellence, new employees, contractors or suppliers perceive that the company will accept lower standards and poor work, as this seems to be the norm.

## The Danger of Regression

Almost all change programmes start off with the introduction of a plethora of activities, and are fanfared with a powerful communication of the strategic plan for the process.

In my experience, almost all of these high-profile change plans suffer from severe regression, and all the well-intended initiatives and activities gradually become marginalised by the pressures of normal day-to-day work. This leads to a gradual loss of momentum in the programme, and also causes individuals who were initially convinced that the plan was necessary to become disillusioned with its progress, as do those who sponsored and championed its introduction.

To avoid this regression, gradual introduction of key enabling initiatives that incrementally improve performance and help to create the new desired culture is required. These initiatives can be viewed as 'pit-props', akin to supports for a new tunnel, preventing it from collapsing, and they will similarly avoid the disintegration of the change plan. This is illustrated by the diagram below.

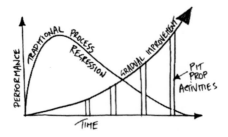

| KEY MESSAGES |
|---|
| • Excellence is a mindset, not a process |
| • Identify core business processes and enablers and set excellence standards for each |
| • Assess the current state for each excellence category and design initiatives to move towards excellence |
| • Implement a zero-tolerance approach |
| • Beware of regression, and gradually introduce 'pit-props' to support the change |

# 11

## FINALLY

I hope you have enjoyed reading this book, and that you have learned something from my own experiences. All I have sought to do is provide some ideas and concepts as food for thought so that you can implement collaborative working and produce truly high performance collaborative teams. There are no shortcuts. You certainly won't get there by a slavish adherence to either theory or the application of snake-oil techniques.

As you will hopefully have seen from this book, attaining excellent world-class performance standards is much more about people than processes. It's about engendering an organisational culture where people can flourish and grow, and truly fulfil their potential. In today's modern world, organisations cannot be limited by geographical boundaries; people need to interact freely with each other and then collaboration will become the norm.

Collaboration will make organisations more open so that everyone associated with the company, be they employees or service providers, will actively look for opportunities to continually improve performance.

New ideas will no longer be the province of managers alone, but will become a distillation of the best of everyone's ideas.

To collaborate effectively you need to have an inquisitive and open mind, so remember not to protect your position but to learn from others.

And really finally – if you would like to contact me to continue our own collaborative discussion my email is paulwilliams@wcgcollaboration.com

Lightning Source UK Ltd.
Milton Keynes UK
UKOW04f1642280815

257715UK00003B/27/P